The Productive INTP

Paul Q. Peters

CONTENTS

- INTRODUCTION 1
  - Warning: An MBTI-Heavy Discussion 3
  - The Cognitive Stack 3
  - Advice and Its Problems 4
  - Sources That Have Influenced Me 6
  - What I've Done So Far 7
  - Structure and Summary 12
- CHAPTER 1: ON FREEDOM AND DISCIPLINE 15
  - What Is Reality? 16
  - The Freedom to Choose Not to Choose 17
  - Charles Crumb 19
  - Reality Continued 21
  - The Law of Entropy 24
  - Freedom and Discipline Reversed 25
  - Leaving Our Captivity 28
  - The Ones and Zeros Around It All 31
- CHAPTER 2: ON PURPOSE, INTERESTS, AND OBSESSIONS 33
  - Seeking Meaning, Finding Nihilism 35
  - Avoid the Ti Si Loop of Death—the Pursuit of Absolute Certainty 39
  - Breaking out of the Loop and into the Extroverted Intuition 41
  - Interests and Obsessions 43
  - Circumambulation 45
  - The Process of the Pursuit 49
  - Others and Your Interests 52
  - Conclusion 54
- CHAPTER 3: ON HABITS 56
  - Aristotle on Habits 58
  - The Efficiency of Habits 59
  - The Nature of Habit 61
  - Habits with Goals 63
  - Breaking Habits 65
  - Time and New Habits 68

Tracking Habits 71
Think Big with Small Steps 72

CHAPTER 4: ON ENERGY MANAGEMENT, PART 1 76

Energy Management > Time Management 76
The Nature of Ne 79
The Energy Matrix 81
The Religion of Diets 85
Energy and Food 88
Sleep and Energy 92
Strategies for Sleep 95

CHAPTER 5: ON ENERGY MANAGEMENT, PART 2 98

Exercise 98
On Meditation 103
A Brief History 103
Benefits 105
Why Does It Work? 107
The Exercise 109
Other Options in the Matrix 112
The Wim Hof Method 113
Strategies for Naps 114
The Energy Matrix Revisited 116

CHAPTER 6: ON TIME MANAGEMENT 118

The Problem with Scheduling 119
Si and Predictability 121
Ne and Possibilities 122
Chaos and Order 124
Start with a Vision 125
Ne and Si Together 126
Tiny Steps 128
Where to Keep Your List 128
Scheduling Summary 130

INTRODUCTION

So, you're an INTP and you want to be productive ... but hold on a second. Isn't that a contradiction? A productive INTP? Seriously? Aren't INTPs lazy? Why would someone like you flirt with the idea of reading a book like this one?

At one level, I do believe that INTPs are lazy. We can go ahead and pat ourselves on the back and say, "No, we're not. We just like to think a lot. We have very active minds!" But this is one of the reasons why I constantly think about throwing the entire MBTI out the window, because I'm not sure if it helps or if gives people like us allowance for excuses. The fact that I keep scoring as an INTP gives me the right to sit around and ruminate for eternity. But honestly, I find that INTPs don't share this sentiment. I believe that every INTP has a hidden desire to dream big dreams as we lay in our beds till 12 pm or 3 pm the next day, thinking about life and its possibilities.

I believe that, like me, many INTPs are struggling to learn how to produce more—and to do this more efficiently. They have a sense that they really aren't as stupid as they feel. They just have to find a different way of getting things done because the old-fashioned way of doing things, the Te way of "just doing it" eludes us. I can hear Shia LaBeouf in my head. "Just do it!" The Nike sign swoops

Introduction

in. Words appear under the Nike symbol, giving me a philosophy about life that uses the economy of three words: "Just do it." But ... but ... but how? And that's the point of this book.

I learned about the Myers-Briggs Type Indicator a while ago, in college, and have been secretly obsessing about it ever since. I have observed myself and my own frustrations with productivity and have felt alone in the endeavor. I felt weird because I seemed to dream bigger than most of the people around me but at the same time, I did less than most people. Big ideas were brewing in my head, but my execution of those ideas was worse than that of the people around me, the ones who didn't seem to dream at all. I lay in bed for hours, staring into the Mirror of Erised, gazing at my "deepest, most desperate desire of our hearts" while doing nothing. Dumbledore whispers, "It does not do to dwell on dreams and forget to live, remember that." I know this, but what am I supposed to do about these ideas? Just throw them away and grow up like everyone else, huh? Thanks. Haven't heard that one before.

I have ambitions, but these ambitions aren't carrying me forward. So, in the past, I've turned to numerous self-help books for advice on execution. I've also turned to the MBTI to help me understand myself and why these recurring themes are in my life. If you're wondering what this book is about, that's basically it. It's a self-help, self-understanding book. And that's basically what I'm saying. If that's the kind of book you're interested in, or a book that you could use at this point in your life, then that's what I've attempted to write.

I want to answer the question: How do we get those seemingly lazy INTPs out into the world and actually *do* things?

Warning: An MBTI-Heavy Discussion

First, a little warning and a little education. The first time I heard people talk about the MBTI, I was utterly confused. After learning my type, I was somewhat interested. I wanted to learn more, to see if there was anything to it, or if it was just another one of those horoscope astrology things. I searched the universe of YouTube and found two people talking, using words and phrases in combinations that made the English language sound like an anchient East African tounge. "The Ti helps sharpen the Ne while Si sits in the background providing information and data for the Ti to … You don't want the Ne getting out of control…"

I kept listening, waiting for the moment when I would go, "Aha! I get it. Now those words make sense." But it never happened … at least not until I went far down the rabbit hole of the MBTI, when I learned about the cognitive stack and how cognitive functions work together. I'm saying all this as a warning, because I wrote this little book through the lens of the cognitive stack of an INTP. So if you're not familiar with MBTI language, you may find the book to be a little difficult at first.

The Cognitive Stack

I have an audience in mind. I've heard that INTPs make up 2% of the population. Whatever the percentage, that is my audience for

Introduction

this book. But really, the audience is even smaller. Out of that population, I want to talk to those who wish to become more productive and efficient. So if you don't know anything about the cognitive stack I'm going to summarize it specifically for the INTP, but feel free to further investigate.

The resources that have most helped me understand the stack are the good people running the world of personalityhacker: Antonia Dodge and Joel Mark Witt. They came up with a car model that exceeds all other metaphors for understanding the stack of each type. The car model has four people riding along, each representing a cognitive function: 1) The Driver, 2) The Co-Pilot, 3) The Ten-Year-Old, and 4) The Three-Year-Old.

For the INTP, the stack goes like this: Ti-Ne-Si-Fe. They drive with an accuracy function called "introverted thinking": Ti. The Co-Pilot is the exploration function extroverted intuition: Ne. The Ten-Year-Old in the back seat is the memory function called "introverted sensing": Si. The last function, The Three-Year-Old, is called "harmony," or, specifically, "extroverted feeling": Fe.

I will be referring to each function throughout this book, so if you're still lost, I would highly recommend listening to a podcast or watching videos from personalityhacker, or reading their articles to better understand the modes of thinking in which INTPs generally find themselves.

Advice and Its Problems

I have read many self-help books, which have helped with some areas in which I am trying to improve. But there's a problem I keep running into as I read the advice of very smart and productive people. They seem to give advice from and for their own type. Even if they try to stretch their techniques and principles to fit a wider audience, they still slip their personal-type biases into their advice, whether they know it or not.

Here's an example. You've probably seen Tony Robbins on YouTube or read a book by him. I am 95% sure the guy is an ENFJ. I'm not going to state why I think he's an ENFJ, but the guy's Fe is off the charts. If you don't recognize the name, I suggest watching the documentary *I Am Not Your Guru*. I've read two of his books and on my shelf is a book that is just a summary of all his ideas.

He gives this advice: "If you're in your head you're dead." It's a principle he uses for everyone, but it seems that the advice comes from an ENFJ's natural disposition. They suppress introverted thinking, so the advice doesn't seem to come from a place of wisdom but of repression. Introverted thinking is very difficult for ENFJs, just like extroverted feeling is naturally very difficult for INTPs.

Before writing this book, I read several biographies of individuals who many believe are INTPs, like Abraham Lincoln and Albert Einstein, the two biggest names of the bunch. In their biographies, the writers talk about how much time these men spent in solitude and in their own heads. Tony Robbins' advice to Abraham Lincoln and Albert Einstein would have been to stop being in their heads so much. "If you're in your head, you're dead." I've been told many times that I think too much, but I've never been told this by another thinking type, especially another INTP.

Introduction

This is the problem with advice from anyone, which is the basis of any self-help book. Your type will change the style, structure, and content of the advice given. I think I could give good advice to an INFP, but I don't think I have the style or structure that would come across to an INFP.

I am an INTP who has struggled to be as productive as I wish to be. In the past, I looked for help and advice from other self-help books, but then learned about the MBTI. I secretly desired a "how-to-be-productive" book made specifically for INTPs but couldn't find one. So I wrote one with the cognitive stack in mind. What is the best advice for an INTP? What is bad advice? Which principles seem to align better with the INTP's natural disposition? I wish to answer these questions through the lens of the INTP cognitive stack.

Sources That Have Influenced Me

Here's a list of some of the sources that have consciously influenced this book:

Deep Work
The Power of Full Engagement
The Tim Ferriss Podcast
Optimize with Brian Johnson
David Perlmutter's Books
Spark: The Revolutionary New Science of Exercise and the Brain
The Happiness Advantage
The Happiness Hypothesis
Twelve Rules for Life
Driven to Distraction

Unlimited Power
Awaken the Giant Within
Moonwalking with Einstein
The Talent Code
Why We Sleep: Unlocking the Power of Sleep and Dreams

Throughout the book, I will refer to these resources because they've helped me tremendously. My goal is to synthesize the principles that best fit the INTP personality type.

What I've Done So Far

So, who am I to discuss this very important topic? What have I done that gives me the right to write this book? For one, as an INTP, I really don't care much about authority figures. If what you say is true, who cares what certificates of achievement hang on your wall? *I'm a doctor in...* Doctors are wrong all the time, while regular people can hold truths that doctors don't seem to see.

I'm just saying to say I'm not someone with lofty ideas, discussing them purely on a conceptual level. Rather, I'm someone who struggled early in life to get things done, to become successful during my second try at college, to get a decent job, learn to write code, write some novels (one is actually sitting on my shelf right now; so far, I've completed around 20 short stories and written a play and two movie scripts), blah, blah, blah. My stomach is turning as I write this stuff down. I just want to make the point

Introduction

that I am in life's game with you, attempting to figure it out. I'm not the most productive person in the world. I'm not trying to stand on a hill and say, "Come follow me. I will show you the way." I'm simply someone who has fought my own laziness and, while many times I have lost that battle, there have been times when I have won.

I remember the first time I had homework that I didn't want to do. I was four years old. I had been doing homework for a while but only because I wanted to. This time, for some reason (I don't know what the homework was exactly), my mother gave me a piece of paper to complete and I didn't care for it. I was in the kitchen and she said I had to complete it. I had to do it. The words were foreign to me. Honestly, they still are. I *had* to do something? It was insane. I didn't understand. Why did I have to do something that I didn't want to do? I couldn't wrap my head around the idea. But my mother said I couldn't do anything until the homework was finished.

I went downstairs, into the basement, with this horrible feeling in my stomach. I could feel it, in that moment: the world around me was changing drastically. I can't remember if I finished the homework but I remember crying my eyes out. It was painful, but I was moving into a world where I would have to do things even if I didn't want to. I still remember the story vividly, because I'm still that little crying child, wanting to stay in a world where I do things only because I want to do them.

I grew up but didn't change. I struggled in school and was almost held back in my seventh-grade year because of my grades—a very embarrassing moment in my life. I did fine in math, but anything that required reading, I failed. English, history, social studies, anything in which the teacher said, "Go home and read X amount of pages," I failed. Eventually, I finished high school and went to college, only to withdraw from all my classes at the end of the first semester. I was failing all of them except physics.

Feeling down, not sure what to do with my life, I went to a recruiter's office and signed up for the military, the US Army. After completing the contract, I mainly asked questions about college, so I wouldn't have to pay for it. Yes, I was one of those recruits. I was in it for the college, which is strange because I did worse in high school than many people who didn't want a higher education.

My entire life, I've had the desire to learn, but on my own terms. I improved at reading, though I'm not the greatest or the fastest. In fact, I think I'm slower than the average reader, which I think is normal for INTPs. Abraham Lincoln and Albert Einstein both struggled with reading. Before I knew about the MBTI, I looked up ways to focus while reading and I learned their techniques. Abraham Lincoln would read words or mumble the words on the page out loud. Einstein would sit with a piece of paper next to him and, if his mind ever wandered, make a tick mark on the paper. He would say to himself, "I will not think of that again," and then keep reading.

After the military, I went back to college and got a degree in English Literature. I never paid much attention to my grades in high school or college. I saw other students around me calculating their grades and seeing what grade they would need in their current class to keep their scholarship or get on the dean's list or whatever. I never did that because I had the G.I. Bill, plus I always

Introduction

thought grades were ridiculous. Grades aren't for the student but for everyone else to decide whether the student is worthy, or how worthy they are. I ended up with a 3.7 GPA, Summa Cum Laude, which is a little funny in light of the fact that I failed all my English classes throughout high school.

Online, people make a big deal about INTPs and their intelligence, that they're all geniuses. I, however, don't feel that way about myself. In fact, I'm a little insecure about my intelligence. IQ is a measurement of how fast someone can learn, but my entire life I have felt that I learn slowly. I've read online—on forums or in YouTube comments—that other INTPs feel this way, too. Abraham Lincoln felt the same way about himself. A lot of people thought he was a genius, but also a lot of people did not. He said of himself that he learned quite slowly. This comforts me because I don't feel so alone about feeling stupid. I think it's normal for INTPs to secretly feel this way about themselves.

After college, you can't do much with a liberal arts degree. Whenever I hear someone make a joke about people with liberal arts degrees, I laugh at myself and say, "Yep, that's me." Except all the liberal arts students who complain. I've never complained about my liberal arts degree and lack of prospects because of it. I didn't get the degree because of the jobs available afterward. I got it simply because I wanted to, and because I'm still that little kid crying in the basement, wanting to do things simply because he wants to do them.

That said, a few months after graduating from college, I thought to myself: *I need to get a better job.* At this time, through school, I had learned about the MBTI and personality types. I had learned that INTPs make good computer programmers, and programming computers had always been an interesting idea to me. I came across a website that offered a free curriculum teaching skills in HTML, CSS, and JavaScript. At the end of the program, one would have knowledge of about nine software applications. With no prior programming experience, I took six months to make my own website and nine apps.

After making the website, I got a few interviews with software companies, which was a little scary. Six months earlier, I never would have been interviewed by the companies. Now, I was being judged by programmers who had been in the field for decades, and I had learned about creating functions only a few months earlier. Eventually, I got a job, not in programming but in the world of cryptocurrency and blockchain technology, which are both beautiful concepts to me.

I worked with Excel sheets all day and eventually used what I had learned about programming to code my daily audits. Eventually, my managers caught wind of what I was doing. They told me that I didn't have to do any of my jobs anymore but that I should keep programming everyone's Excel sheets for them. When I started, four people were doing audits. After 95% of everything was automated, only one person was needed to complete the daily audits.

Basically, they wanted me to automate everything I could, so I did that for about two months. They threw me around the company. I went into different departments that I didn't know about and programmed mindless processes so that they became automated. Eventually, the programming team caught wind of what I was

Introduction

doing and brought me into their department. Now I work as a full-time software engineer.

I say this simply to show that I am not your genius, mythical INTP, as well as to show that I've had to work to get things done. I'm not your most accomplished INTP; far from it. I failed a lot growing up, in elementary school, middle school, junior high, high school, and college. But I think I've struggled enough with learning and being productive to at least begin writing a book about the personality type and how to be a productive one. Most, if not all, of these ideas aren't my own, but a synthesis of ideas I have accumulated over the years. So, let's get into it. I want to start with the question: Why, in the first place, would someone like you want to be productive?

Structure and Summary

Chapter 1: On Freedom and Discipline

This chapter is mainly a long essay on the relationship between freedom and discipline. I try to drill deep into the ideas, to help wrap my head around it. It's basically a long, meandering philosophical essay. I desire freedom, which is really the whole point of this book: to free myself to pursue the things I wish to pursue. I basically try to help myself, and you, understand why there are some things in life we must do even if we don't want to do them. I try to make sense of it through a heavy Ti discussion.

Chapter 2: On Purpose, Interests, and Obsessions

This is another essay that discusses interests and purposes. It's about how to look for interests if you don't have any, and why they are important. It also deals with the nihilism that INTPs seem to naturally fall into, and how to get out of those deathly spin cycles. The chapter tries to convince you, and me, to allow an interest to take over and to pursue the interest—a very Ne process.

Chapter 3: On Habits

This chapter is basically about habits: how to break bad ones and create good ones. It may not make a lot of sense if you don't read the first chapter. Habits are largely an Si function endeavor. So, as you can see, the first chapter is Ti-heavy, the second is Ne, and this chapter deals with the Si function.

Chapter 4: On Energy Management, Part 1

This chapter and the next, I would say, are the most important chapters of the book. The first couple chapters deal with why you want to be productive even if you don't want to be. They are sort of warnings. But this gets more into the how. It's all about energy management. I introduce an idea called the Energy Matrix to help you gauge and improve your energy.

Chapter 5: On Energy Management, Part 2

This chapter is just a continuation of energy management. It deals specifically with exercise and meditation, and then presents a few extra ideas to help improve your energy.

Chapter 6: On Time Management

Introduction

This chapter is about scheduling and why it's difficult, as an INTP, to schedule your day. I offer some solutions to the problem. However, I would advise you to learn energy management before you learn how to manage your time. This discipline is a lot harder to learn if you don't have any energy. If you learn the habits in Chapters 4 and 5, managing your time will become much, much easier.

CHAPTER 1:
ON FREEDOM AND DISCIPLINE

"Through discipline comes freedom."
—Aristotle

Deep down, I find that what's most difficult in terms of being productive, for myself and other INTPs, is the desire for freedom and autonomy. I have a hard time finishing tasks because new ideas come to mind that I wish to pursue. Dr. A. J. Drenth has taught me a great deal through his blog posts and books on INTPs. He says, "The INTP personality type is the most independent and philosophical of all the 16 types. INTPs have a deep need for personal autonomy and independence of thought." [1] I agree with this statement 100%.

However, Aristotle has a prophetic saying. I'm not sure what type Aristotle was; people online think ENTJ, which may be true. Jocko Willink has come across the same idea in his books, *Extreme Ownership* and the recent *Discipline Equals Freedom*. I'm 95% positive that Jocko Willink is an ESTJ. Whatever their types may be, there does seem to be something about discipline and freedom—like a relationship between them.

On Freedom and Discipline

Discipline is something I have a hard time wrapping my head around. After all these years, I still don't understand why I have to do something when I don't want to do it. I still haven't accepted a world in which you need to do things because you have to do them. It's too simple. It seems more like a manipulative tactic of those who wish to control me.

But, okay, fine. Freedom to choose, freedom to pursue the things and ideas I want and that spark my interest. Aristotle is telling me that I can have the freedom if I follow through with the discipline. Jocko Willink is telling me that freedom and discipline are the same thing—at least, that's the title of the book, though I don't think he believes that. They both say this is the reality around life itself. But is it? What is the reality surrounding the ideas of freedom and discipline?

What Is Reality?

One of my favorite authors, Philip K. Dick, in his essay, "How to Build a Universe That Doesn't Fall Apart Two Days Later," said, "Reality is that which, when you stop believing in it, doesn't go away." At first glance, I really like that saying. I have thought about it a lot over the years, using it as a sort of heuristic for myself. When people say things like, "I believe this is true," I think to myself, 'You may believe that's true, but would it still be there if you ceased to believe it?' If the answer is a satisfactory yes, I think the person is on to something.

Right now, in quantum mechanics, what we believe about reality is changing rapidly. The question "Does the tree make a sound if no one is there to hear it?" has been around since forever—at least it seems that way to me. But in quantum mechanics, there is such a thing as a superposition in which things may or may not be there depending upon our perception. Schrödinger's cat may be dead in the bunker or it may be alive. There's a thing called the quantum cloud that represents the possibility of where things may be before we perceive them, as atoms lie in a superposition. So, the new questions that should be asked in philosophy now are: "Is the tree even there before we look at it? Does it go away if we cease to perceive it?"

I asked the same of Aristotle and his idea. He believes that discipline and freedom are related, specifically describing their relation through a process. Discipline comes first and, through it, freedom arises. This is another way to say it—probably a wordier version of "through discipline comes freedom." Jocko Willink believes they are the same thing, that they are equivalent. They both believe it to be true, and you may believe it to be true, but is the idea still there when we cease to believe it?

So, I asked the questions: What is the reality revolving around freedom? Specifically, the freedom to choose my pursuits and be who I want? Does the relationship between freedom and discipline go away if I turn my back on it? Can I again live in the world in which I do things only because I wish to do them? Can I return to my four-year-old self and have the freedom I desire?

The Freedom to Choose Not to Choose

As of the time of this book's writing, I'm thirty years old and people have stopped asking me the question, "What do you want to be when you grow up?" People stopped asking that question when I got a job after graduating from college. In college, when I told people that I was getting a degree in English literature, they would ask me, "So, are you gonna teach? What are you going to do with that?" Frankly, I never knew and I still don't. I had ideas, thousands of them, but nothing ever stuck with a loud, decisive, "That's it! That's what I'll do!"

Before college, I watched the show "House" and wanted to be a medical doctor. I went to the library by myself, opening up books about anatomy and any book that seemed to be a part of the curriculum for med school. After a week, I got bored and moved on to something else. I first went to college to work on airplanes as a mechanic but did horribly in class. I liked learning about only the physics of airplanes, so I quit and joined the military. I never quite figured out what I wanted to do in the military after my contract was complete. When I got out and jumped into the world of the university, I took general eds with the idea of becoming a physical therapist, though I wasn't really sure why. I think it was because physical therapists were in high demand. But that fell through.

I liked reading, even though I was slow, so I decided to go with English literature, against the advice of many family members and friends. I could never find the one thing that brought together all my interests. A big reason why I liked English literature was that it kept my options open. What does one do with a bachelor's in English literature? Honestly, no one really knows. You either continue your education and become a professor, or work as a copywriter, or work at Home Depot as a manager. In my case, I was working at a hotel as a night auditor when I finished and then became the front desk manager not long after that. It was emotionally exhausting to deal with customers all day and to make sure the employees I managed were doing their jobs.

You may be asking, "Why do all that if you hated it?" I would have to say, "That's a very good question." I got married during college, which increased my responsibility, so I had to bring home a little more money. The walls around me were closing. The freedom to not choose was choosing my life for me.

Charles Crumb

I've listened to just about all of Jordan Peterson's lectures. I'm sure you've heard of him. His star to fame rose very rapidly. In one of his lectures online, he mentions a documentary called *Crumb*, about underground artist Robert Crumb. The film focuses on his career in the 1960s and 1970s. In the film, Robert Crumb didn't capture my interest so much as his brother, Charles Crumb, did. The man is the pinpoint definition of an INTP and the film portrayed an image of him that scared me. He reminded me a lot of myself and what I would become later in life. He was in his late 40s during the making of the film.

Throughout the movie, Charles lives with his mother in a top-floor bedroom. He's 48 or 49. At first glance, his set-up doesn't seem so bad. In fact, I've described a desire to live a similar lifestyle. In the past, I thought it wouldn't be all that bad if, somehow, I ended up in solitary confinement, trapped in prison, but could have all the books I wanted, when I wanted them, and as many notepads and pens as I needed. You see, what I really want isn't that exact situation, but the ability to read when I want to read, and to think about the things I want to think about when I want to think about them. Charles Crumb had that while living with his mother.

His appearance was depressing. Looking at him, I could feel depression seep under my skin. His head was overly large and his hair was unkempt. He had a round face with large, sweaty cheeks, and his lower jaw protruded in an underbite. his teeth were meshed together and dirty and not all there. Listening to him talk and interact with his brother gave me the chills. There was something very familiar about him. He was who I would have been if I lived in a different world, similar to his, where I was allowed to choose the paths of least resistance, I would have ended up just like he did. At times in my life when I pull away from my dreams and ambitions and walk a path pulled by the energy of my vices, I start to morph. My cheeks grow, my depression worsens, and I metamorphose into a person very similar to—almost exactly like—him.

At the end of his life, his vices held him captive. He couldn't escape. Freedom closed around him. He couldn't leave the house and had to stay in his room with his books scattered everywhere. At the time of the movie, he couldn't even get an erection, which would have provided a small window of escape from his depressing situation. He took antidepressants, which I would, too, if I lived like he did. I think anyone would. But his room, his mother, his books, his antidepressants, his flaccid member—in the end, none of that worked for him. When the movie was over and as the credits moved up the screen, a text read that Charles Crumb had committed suicide not long after the making of the documentary.

You may be thinking that I'm being quite harsh with the man. He's gone and I'm never going to interact with his family. But it's not him I'm being harsh with, exactly. It's me. I know him very well, even though I've never met him. Online, on YouTube, people complain about how difficult it is being an INTP, but then there's this other side where we worship ourselves for being in a group of very intelligent, very interesting people, like Abraham Lincoln or Albert Einstein or whoever. The truth, I believe, is that people like us either live life very well or crash hard. Yes, there are great people who had a personality type similar to mine, but there are also people whose very appearance depresses me, and we're all in the same pool of losers.

Reality Continued

Morpheus asks Neo, "What is real? How do you define real? If you're talking about what you can feel, what you can smell, what you can taste and see, then real is simply electrical signals interpreted by your brain."

I'm not asking this question to sound mysterious or interesting. Most people, I believe, who ask "What is real" or "What is truth?" are disingenuous. They aren't interested in pursuing the question, but I am.

Last year, I read a book by Charles Petzold called *Code: The Hidden Language of Computer Hardware and Software*. I was learning how to program and I heard from several people online that this was a seminal book all programmers should read. I was also interested in learning how computers turn electricity into digestible information on a screen. The book goes over the history of how computers were made, from simple Morse code devices to the PCs we use today.

In it, I learned a concept that I've carried with me ever since, and probably will for the rest of my life, even if I never code again. As many know, and probably most INTPs know, computers interpret binary code that produces everything we see on the screen. For example, the capital letter A is read as 01000001 in binary. As a traditional numeric value, the capital letter A is the number 65. Computers are reading hundreds, thousands, millions, billions of these electrical currents, made by ones and zeros, to produce everything on the screen and all the information in the background. Currently, I'm writing this book using the program Microsoft Word, which represents billions of zeros and ones. However, inside the context of Microsoft Word's zeros and ones is a small set of ones and zeros, the 01000001 representing every capital letter A on the screen inside the Microsoft Word program.

So, what is really producing the capital letter A? The 01000001? Or the context of the Microsoft Word program? Of course, this isn't an "either/or" answer, but a "both/and" answer. From this idea, we can extrapolate a greater principle. To know the truth about anything, you must know the thing itself and the context that surrounds it. So. I asked the question: "What is real?" What I really need to know is something I want to know and the context surrounding that thing.

Here's an example. Everyone online makes fun of flat earthers. However, knowing the context of the question "Is the earth flat or not?" changes the answer to either a "yes" or a "no." If I look outside my window right now, the world looks flat to me. If I go out to the fields and look at the horizon, it spreads across on a flat line. From that perspective, the earth isn't a globe but a flat surface. But, of course, you may say that I have the wrong perspective. The right perspective is to look at Earth from outer space, which would make the earth a globe. But what if we back up the perspective even farther? What if we go to the edge of the universe, to the event horizon?

A professor at Stanford University, Leonard Susskind, worked with Stephen Hawking on the nature of black holes. From his research, he believes that the universe may be a hologram. What we may be experiencing is what our images have produced from the edge of the universe. I'm not saying this is true, but I find it interesting. And if it is true, everything in the universe is a flat surface. The projection of the light makes the hologram. If the holographic theory is true, and that becomes our new context (the ones and zeros that surround the question of the nature of Earth's flatness), the earth becomes flat again. I look out my window and the earth is flat. I look at the Earth from a satellite and the earth is a globe. I look at the Earth from the boundary of space and it's flat again.

What I'm saying is, the ones and zeros surrounding the question change the answer. The context and the thing surrounded by the context create reality.

In *The Matrix*, when Cipher is eating at the restaurant, he lifts up the steak, stares at it, and says, "You know, I know the steak doesn't exist." But his conclusion isn't exactly true. It depends on whether the question is asked inside the ones and zeros of the matrix or outside of it. He's inside the matrix when he says the statement, but he's probably thinking about the world outside of it. Because he's inside the context of the matrix, I would say the

On Freedom and Discipline

steak does, in fact, exist. But, of course, I can understand why he believes the steak isn't real. And I would concede to anyone who accepts the opposite conclusion as my own.

The Law of Entropy

So, what happened to Charles Crumb? Essentially, I believe entropy happened to him. Entropy is simply the measuring tool of the second law of thermodynamics. To simply summarize the second law of thermodynamics, when matter moves freely throughout the universe, or as energy changes from one state to another, disorder increases. By default, life sucks and because of the second law of thermodynamics, the suckiness increases as time passes. As we sit and twiddle our thumbs, pondering the meaning of life, the world around us, by default, gets suckier. The proverbial walls around us close. Freedom slowly dissipates, evaporating into a state of nothingness.

As a thought experiment, imagine that you did nothing for three months to combat the second law of thermodynamics. The only exceptions would be to eat, drink, and go to the bathroom. If I sat here and did nothing for the next three months, my relationship with my wife would change into a completely disordered state. Every day, I must impose my will into the relationship to keep it functioning. However, if I did nothing for three months, my wife would hate me. I don't know if she'd divorce me, but she'd definitely think about it. My workplace would fire me. The bills would pile up, and we'd have to move from our house, and probably move in with her parents (though I'm not sure they'd let me if I decided to become a vegetable for three months). My own personal world would get very sucky. I would definitely gain weight. Any sort of in-shape-ness I currently have would fall apart. Depression would almost certainly take over my consciousness. If I don't exercise and eat well (especially if I eat too much sugar), I get depressed very quickly.

I'm not sure what would happen exactly, but I know entropy would increase because, well, that's just the universe. By default, life sucks and its suckiness increases as time passes.

Did the same thing happen to Charles Crumb? He seemed to find a way around it. He made his universe very small, living alone with his mom inside that small room of his. What would happen if he conducted the same thought experiment? I'm not sure. He'd last much longer than I would because there was less in his life to fall apart. Yet even the small section of the universe he'd carved out for himself got smaller. He still didn't escape the second law of thermodynamics. Freedom slowly dissipated and captivity took over his life to the point where he could think of only one way to escape the suckiness of it all. The ones and zeros of our universe change into a suckier state if we don't interact with it. What Aristotle discovered was that the relationship between freedom and discipline doesn't seem to go away even if a person refuses to believe it.

Freedom and Discipline Reversed

Freedom through discipline works, and as we've seen, so does discipline through freedom. It seems to work both ways. One of the assumptions of mathematics is its symmetry, which is an assumption that proves itself right over and over again. What happens when you add positive 4 to positive 4? You get 8. What about adding negative 4 to negative 4? You get negative 8. If the universe was reversed, as in, it was held up to a mirror, everything would work exactly the same. So, what about this principle that Aristotle discovered?

If we choose freedom now, do we get discipline later? Of course, the answer is yes. There are many different ways we can look at the question or rephrase the principle. Through discipline comes freedom. But another way to say it is "through indulgence comes captivity." Or "through permissiveness come slavery." Or perhaps we could flip-flop the concepts of freedom and discipline entirely and say "through freedom comes discipline."

We can look at Charles Crumb's life as an example. In the documentary, he had several chances to choose a life path different from the one that led him to suicide. He was a talented artist and writer. He was given the chance to try out for a magazine. They sent him pages to draw on and gave him instructions to follow, but instead of following the instructions, he made a joke out of the situation. The drawings he sent back were completely insane—weird, small circles that created a dress on the cartoon figures.

He chose the freedom of the path of least resistance, never getting a job and staying home with his mom and with his books in his room. You can tell by looking at him that he chose the freedom to not exercise and to not eat healthily. He then chose the freedom to use antidepressants to help fight back the depression. The more he chose to indulge, the more the walls of life shrank around him to the point where nothing worked for him, so he did the last thing you can do.

I look at my own life through the lens of freedom and discipline, and the same thing happens. As a child, how long was I held captive by the homework my mother gave me? I'm not sure how long it would've taken me, but I'll say ten minutes. I could've gone downstairs and worked through the problem immediately, but instead I chose to cry and pout about it, hoping that would set me free. It didn't. The homework held me prisoner for possibly hours, which has been my story throughout high school and college. I've been held prisoner by homework for countless hours throughout my entire life.

In college, I failed one class. It was speech class. I had been doing fine throughout the course, getting good grades on the tests and speeches. But I completely skipped the last speech—the final one and the one that was worth the most points. I didn't prepare a speech and was instead going to use a speech that a friend gave to me. Before class, I looked over the speech and realized I had no idea what to say if I got up in front of the other students with this speech that my friend had delivered about roller coasters. So I skipped it and failed the class.

Well, it's just a speech class, right? It was a learning experience. True, there are many different ways to look at it but the principles of entropy, freedom, and discipline still hold true. Because I chose the freedom to not prepare a speech, I wasn't able to complete the course, which I would consider discipline. I was held back because I decided not to enter the natural chaotic state of the universe and to create a speech out of it. I was held back, held prisoner, because I did nothing.

Leaving Our Captivity

Now let's flip things again. We should know, by examining our lives through the lens of a lack of discipline, that choosing freedom now leads to a life in which possibilities disappear on their own. I don't want that, and I assume you don't want that, either. The INTP thinks in a world of possibilities to exercise the Ne cognitive function. Extroverted intuition is always thinking, 'What's possible?' And it needs freedom to think that. So, let's turn the table, flip the coin, turn things around, say, "Hello from the other side," and ask the question, "How do we get the freedom we desire?" How free do you want to be? You want to be free, but you don't know how to do it. You agree with me that your lack of discipline has made life gradually suckier, and as you look into the future, things are only going to get worse. But now you wish to reverse your destiny. You no longer want to be held captive.

I want to examine a story from the Bible. I am a Christian, but you don't have to be a Christian to believe the truth behind the stories of the Bible. I believe humans are primarily story creatures, as in, learning from stories is our primary mode of making sense of the world, and not memorizing atemporal facts from scientific books. Though reading scientific books is helpful, a person must be trained in how to do it. For some reason, we learn from and remember stories way more efficiently and effectively than we do scientific literature. So, let's look at the story.

Whether or not the story of Moses and the Israelites happened historically isn't the point I'm making, because I want to look at the story allegorically. You're reading this book, and I'm writing it, because I wish to be somewhere different. I want to be in a better place. All self-help books have an underlying promise. They inherently say that you can be in a better place than wherever you are. For some reason, the universe is symmetrical, and mathematics demonstrates this. We've seen and thought about how things gradually worsen if we do nothing, so let's ask the question, "What if we do the opposite?" What if we chose to discipline ourselves and create new, better habits? What would happen?

In Genesis, the story of Moses actually goes back to the story of Joseph saving his family from a famine. In Egypt, Joseph was second-in-command, next in authority behind Pharaoh. He saved his family from a famine and they came to live in the land of Egypt, where they made their home for generations. After a few generations, a Pharaoh came along who didn't know the story of Joseph and why the Israelites were in Egypt, so he decided to enslave the Israelites. The Israelites became comfortable in the affluent land of Egypt and, as their comfort grew, they became enslaved by the very thing that saved them.

They did nothing and the second law of thermodynamics held true even in the ancient world. By default, by doing nothing, they became slaves through their indulgence, and they paid for it, generation after generation. Four hundred years after Joseph, they began to cry out to God for deliverance. You and I are doing the same thing, as you read the words that I'm writing, I'm sure you are crying out for a better place in some way, or at least pondering the possibility of it and weighing the costs.

On Freedom and Discipline

However, the way the Israelites were saved wasn't what they had in mind. When Moses came back to answer the prayers of the Israelites, he attempted several times to speak with Pharaoh to let the Israelites go. As the Israelites tried to leave Egypt, things got worse. The labor increased and they were given less food. Eventually, after ten plagues, the Israelites were allowed to leave the land of slavery, and it would seem the story was over. They left the land that had enslaved them, the land where they had become too comfortable, and were now free to make it on their own in the world. But the story doesn't end there. The Israelites don't go to the Promised Land in a straight line. In fact, I would say that leaving the land of slavery only begins the story.

You read a self-help book and, like all self-help books, it tells you to implement new habits. You decide to leave the land of your bad habits and implement new ones. Everything works out perfectly, right? Of course not. It doesn't. Things get worse. Your being cries out for the old way you used to live, with all the instant freedom and gratification. You are willing to pay the price of slavery. You go back to the land of slavery, here and there, and then try to make your way into the Promised Land, but you can't get there. The shackles of slavery are tight on your wrists and ankles, and the weight of your bad habits keeps you from moving forward.

The Israelites were given bread to eat, manna from heaven. But they didn't like its taste. They wanted to go back to Egypt and eat the meat and the food provided to them there. When the Israelites moved forward and saw the Promised Land and the battles they would have to fight with the giants, they decided it was too much. So, what happened? Did they leave and go back to the land of slavery? No. They stayed in the wilderness and allowed all the men older than twenty to die. It took close to forty years for them to believe they could win the battles to take over the land of promise. Everyone who came out of the land of Egypt and who desired the land of slavery had to die. It was a painful process.

The Ones and Zeros Around It All

So, it doesn't matter whether or not anyone believes in the relationship between discipline and freedom. It's still there. It doesn't go away. The context of freedom and discipline surrounds the entirety of life. You can sit back and reflect on your life, or you can sit back and reflect on someone else's life and examine the relationship. Because Charles chose paths of least resistance, the universe around him closed and his possibilities disappeared until his mind could conjure only one option and he killed himself. A life of freedom and least resistance leads to slavery. And because we live in a universe with symmetrical principles, the opposite is also true. You can view anyone who is successful and see the possibilities open to them, or you can imagine, for yourself, what you would do if you had a million, two, three, four, whatever million dollars. You would have more time to focus on your interests, the freedom to choose your own pursuits.

So, how do we get to the place where we want to be? Old habits must die and new habits must be created. We must create habits that put us on the paths toward better lands. The process of creating new habits is painful. However, either we go through with the process or we allow the suckiness of life to envelop us, and possibilities disappear. The reality around us, by default, is shrinking and getting worse. To kill our bad habits, we must go through a painful process so we can build the habit that will carry us to the Promised Land. This is the reality of freedom. These are the ones and zeroes that encapsulate life, because the relationship between discipline and freedom doesn't seem to go away, even if one stops believing it.

[1] https://personalityjunkie.com/the-intp/

CHAPTER 2:
ON PURPOSE, INTERESTS, AND OBSESSIONS

> *"There is but one truly serious philosophical problem, and that is suicide. Judging whether life is or is not worth living amounts to answering the fundamental question of philosophy. All the rest—whether or not the world has three dimensions, whether the mind has nine or twelve categories—comes afterwards."*
>
> —Albert Camus

In the last chapter, I was a little critical of Charles Crumb and his decision to take his life. In a famous quote, Albert Camus poses the question of suicide. He believes it is the basis of all philosophy, and that we all must wrestle with the question before we pursue interests. It is a question I keep coming back to when searching for meaning or purpose. We don't have to take suicide literally, either. Mindlessly following the crowd is a form of suicide. Why not destroy ourselves and become like everyone else? Why not cease being a person and, instead, join the millions of mindless automatons inhabiting the earth? Isn't following the crowd, not being an actual and real person, a form of suicide? The question

On Purpose, Interests, and Obsessions

of suicide seems to haunt the INTP and demands an answer before moving forward. Otherwise, it lingers close by and reappears whenever a pursuit becomes difficult. The ceaseless questioning, for some reason, eventually comes around a turn and finds the issue of suicide waiting for the INTP. Nothing has any real meaning. Why not commit suicide?

Albert Camus starts his book, *The Myth of Sisyphus*, with the question of suicide. Later, he analyzes the Greek myth about Sisyphus, who is destined, for the rest of his existence, to push a large rock up a mountain to its summit, only to let it fall back to its base. He walks back down the mountain and repeats the process, over and over again, for all eternity. Camus saw modern man living out this fate through the monotony of life, going to factory work and repeating simple but physically difficult tasks. If only one would take just a few moments and ask a few honest questions—and when I say "honest," I mean it in its fullest sense. Why do you do this thing? I find it meaningful. Why? If one keeps asking this question, and if you are an INTP who has gone through your teenage years, you've no doubt wrestled with this question and been immobilized by it.

However, the question has been asked by serious and intelligent inquirers in the past and present, like Camus and others. Camus himself wasn't the first person to ponder the issue. We can go back to the author of Ecclesiastes, who looks over his life's work and the acts throughout his life, the books he has read, the things he has accomplished, and concludes that it was all meaningless. The writer starts the book by saying, "Meaningless! Meaningless!" / says the Teacher. / "Utterly meaningless! / Everything is meaningless." He is an old man during the writing of the ancient book and can't find anything under the sun that will hold value in the greater picture.

Deep down, this is the difficulty that all INTPs face when looking for an interest to pursue. There is a need to connect the task, or interest, to an all-summarizing principle. For instance, I find it difficult to continue writing this book because I'm not sure if it will connect with my own pursuits. As I start the book, I believe it does. It is helping me better understand who I am and where I fit into the big puzzle of life. I hope, in the process, it will help all those in conversation with me. But the doubt seeps into my awareness whenever I leave the idea for too long. Is writing the book meaningful? Is there purpose in it? Honestly, I'm not certain.

Seeking Meaning, Finding Nihilism

Leading with the cognitive function Ti, INTPs are constantly trying to make sense of the world. How does this make sense? How does this fit in with everything else I know? Supplemented by Ne, the INTP's Ti is specifically looking for conceptual accuracy. How does this idea make sense in connection with every other idea I understand and accept? This is why we try to fit everything inside an all-summarizing principle.

Einstein first asked the question when he was young: "What would it be like to ride on a light beam?" This question stayed with him through high school and into his adult life. It was the basis of how he came up with the theory of special relativity. However, he wanted to pull the theory of special relativity into a greater principle and later came up with the theory of general relativity, a theory that made more sense of the forces of the cosmos. Unfortunately, quantum physics came along and showed that Einstein hadn't summarized the physics of the universe. For large objects, general relativity works, but when one moves down to smaller particles, the subatomic kind, the physics of his universe break down.

Einstein was a genius, unlike me, but all INTPs go through this process. How can we make sense of it all? We start by trying to destroy everything with our Ti to see if anything can stand on its own, and we come out with a sort of Cartesian anxiety. Nothing seems to stand except Renee Descartes' axiom, "I think, therefore I am," and even that thought, as Sartre points out, isn't the first step in consciousness, but "There is thinking, so there is awareness," not that the awareness is my own.

I do get some pleasure from destroying ideas, but because I can't find anything solid to hold in my hands, everything loses its meaning. Nihilism is the unavoidable conclusion, which takes us back to the major question of philosophy: suicide.

I may rant and tell others about my struggle with meaning, but I am told that I think too much and that I should stop. I've been told this several times, by several different people. The person who tells me this doesn't understand what they have said. To stop thinking? To stop being? What are they saying? They're telling me to kill myself, to not be me, but to be them or someone else who's controlling them. They want me to die spiritually, to kill myself, which, again, brings us back to the beginning where we ask ourselves about the question of suicide.

I hope you're not looking for complete closure to this question. My only conclusion consciously doesn't make sense because the law of non-contradiction must be broken. You must accept something as an axiom that can't be proven. It's the only way I've been able to move forward. You must accept that life is better than death. Being is better than nonbeing. It's the basic principle of life, which one must accept without looking for anything below the axiom holding it in place.

The person who I have found to dig deeper into these unanswerable nihilistic questions is Jordan Peterson. He has helped me tremendously, though he is a very controversial figure to those who read only other people's hit pieces about him. We can argue and think about the meaning of life and question whether or not it's better to move forward, but the act of being immobile eventually leads to suffering. By the definition I espouse, any form of death—especially any kind of psychological death—is suffering. At different points in my life, I've seen myself and others decide that life has no meaning. Life ends up becoming really sucky and, eventually, dark and grim. When I start to suffer, and as I see others suffer, argumentation loses all its power. I've yet to see anyone argue their way out of being depressed, or out of their suffering.

Recently, I had the privilege of watching my wife give birth to our first child. I could not think of any words, syllogisms, or knockdown arguments to make the pain of childbirth go away—not that I thought one could be found. I'm just making the point that suffering and pain don't seem to listen to argumentation. You and I can't argue with pain, and eventually choosing not to live and not to be eventually leads to suffering. That's Jordan Peterson's paraphrased version of the argument against nihilism. I believe that you and I must contend with it, as in, contend with our own suffering, if we decide to step further into the "Meaningless! Meaningless! Utterly meaningless!" way of thinking.

All arguments from now on begin with this fundamental axiom. When I see people like Charles Crumb, who can't find meaning, I honestly don't know what to say. Because I get it. I understand it. But reading this book, interacting with these ideas, at some level, you must want to move forward and be productive, to accomplish your dreams, goals, whatever. If you want to move forward, you must accept that living is better than dying as a fundamental principle, even though underneath the bedrock is this elusive cloud.

Morpheus is sitting before you in the dirty leather chair, and he says, "Choose the red or blue pill." One says that life is better than death, but it's the harder of the two pills to swallow. Getting it down will be hard enough, and your body will feel it afterward— pain, turmoil, hunger, thirst, and loads and loads of doubt. You will wake up in a desert, away from all the vices that have been holding you captive with all the others dying in an unconscious state. The only other option is the blue pill. It's easy, and it says, "Nothing has any meaning."

You choose the answer every day, but it's time to become aware of how you've been answering the question. Take the blue pill, continue with your life, and become unconscious of the whole thing through drugs and alcohol or porn, or simply follow through with the real philosophical question of "why not commit suicide?" To further interact with this book, to become more productive than you currently are, you must at least logically and fundamentally assume that living is better than dying, whether it's physical or psychological in nature. To do this, you must give up—at least partially—the pursuit of absolute certainty.

Avoid the Ti Si Loop of Death—the Pursuit of Absolute Certainty

All types have an unhealthy side. Everyone has an introverted and an extroverted loop in which they spin around and around. It's very unhealthy for anyone to stay in their default loop for too long. I used to work with an ENFJ, and her default loop was extroverted feeling and extroverted sensing. She wasn't a very introspective person—like, at all. I asked her once what she thought her faults were. (In the back of my mind, I had thought of several for her. I wanted to see if what I thought of would match her own faults.) She looked away for a moment and then said, "Huh, I don't know. I can't think of any faults. Guess I don't know myself very well." Later, she was almost fired for stealing from the cash register but, somehow, she was able to sweet talk my boss into letting her stay.

Every type has its default loop, and an INTP's is the introverted thinking, introverted sensing loop. You probably do this at night when you're really tired. You lie in bed, thinking about the last idea you learned, going over and over and over it in your head. Maybe it's something about the MBTI. I've gone to sleep many nights thinking about different personality types and trying to figure out the concepts of the different cognitive stacks.

In the loop, you go over the thought in your head. It's one you've already stored in your memory, so no real learning is involved.

On Purpose, Interests, and Obsessions

You're just trying to obsessively understand the concept by looking at it through as many perspectives your mind has gathered. You loop through the idea repeatedly. INTPs are generally more scared of NOT being wrong then they are of being right. This over-and-over process in your head is called the Ti Si loop. The Ti is taking your stored memories, Si, and flipping everything around, trying to place already-gathered ideas in the correct spots. It's the pursuit of certainty.

And this is the problem. You aren't getting any new data. The Ne is sitting dormant, wanting to take in new information. The Ti and Si are wanting to clean the data, to make it as conceptually accurate as possible. When INTPs get like this, everyone around them turns into idiots and offers nothing of value. A clear sign that an INTP is unhealthy is that they have to correct people as they talk. I've listened to other feeler types rant, and I can't follow them once they make a contradictory statement, or at least a statement that seems contradictory to me. It's not always a contradiction, but it's always something that doesn't make sense. I want to stop them and make them explain what they meant by whatever came out of their face.

An unhealthy INTP is almost impossible to talk to because they can't take in any new information. I get this way when I'm tired. At a certain point, I don't want to be around anyone if I'm too tired. I end up being dull, a lifeless vegetable around friends and family. It's even worse around new people because I have to travel down the comfortable getting-to-know-someone path with questions like, "What do you like to do for fun?" or "So, how do you know this person we both know?" But an unhealthy INTP will simply not engage in that kind of activity at all.

How do you break out of this Ti Si loop? You simply engage the Ne. Engaging the Ne is also how we move into the world and actually DO things instead of sitting alone in our rooms mulling over the same things over and over again. In the story of Israel, Ne is Moses coming into the land of Egypt and telling the Israelites to leave and enter the wilderness. In the story of Alice in Wonderland, it's the rabbit hole. No one really knows what lies in the desert for you or for me, or what's at the end of the rabbit hole. But that's also why chasing it, or leaving the land of tyranny, is fun. We both don't know what's going to happen but chasing the rabbit hole is better than staying where you are in the Ti Si loop of absolute certainty.

Breaking out of the Loop and into the Extroverted Intuition

So, you want out of the land of slavery and to begin the journey to the land of promise. Well, breaking into Ne isn't all that hard. However, following through with the Ne is the issue. Somehow, you must take in new information. Any way you want. Get out of bed and open a book you've never read, one that has captured your interest for whatever reason. A way to conceptualize Ne is through exploration. Take in new data some way, somehow. INTPs are known for getting obsessed with interests. Obsessions are the gold mines—like the real, actual gold mines for INTPs. However, to the INTP, not all interests are created equal. Some stick around for a very long time, while others seem to come and go with the breeze.

On Purpose, Interests, and Obsessions

I used Einstein as an example earlier, when he was a young teenager imagining what it would be like to ride a beam of light. The question pops into the mind, and says to the INTP, "Explore me, follow this interesting rabbit hole." It may lead to a dead end or to something infinitely fascinating. Einstein listened to the question in his head into his thirties. At some point (I don't know exactly when), the interest developed into an obsession. It took over every faculty in his mind as he pursued the question ruthlessly, almost too much so. The obsession later became the reason why he and his first wife divorced.

If I have one critique for Einstein, it's that he didn't break out of his Ti Si loop of general relativity. It's quite well-known that he was pursuing the big TOE, the theory of everything. However, unfortunately, he was never able to develop new ideas after general relativity was published and mostly accepted. He spent the rest of his several decades of life trying to fit the TOE into his theory but was never able to do so with the new discovery of quantum mechanics. I believe he could have made many more discoveries and advancements toward the TOE if he broke out of his Ti Si loop and moved into his Ne more often.

The point is, the obsession started as a small, innocent question. At the time, Einstein had no idea that the question would take him into a world where he would flip all of cosmology and the way we look at the universe on its head. There's no way he could have seen that. And he made no prophesy that this would happen. He was simply following the question, the Ne, into whatever world it created.

Passions are things I've never been able to understand. I'm not sure if I have any passions or if I've ever had one. I understand

The Productive INTP

only interests and obsessions. I've heard the aphorism, "Follow your passion," which I'm sure you've also heard. But I'm not giving that advice. I'm not sure what it means. I haven't had the chance to ask another INTP if they have passions, or if they understand the notion of a passion. But I have interests—like, a thousand of them.

The interests sometimes snowball into something that takes over my life. It gets to the point where I can no longer talk to people because it's all I think about. I'm at work and people are talking, making conversation about everyday things: he-said, she-said type of stuff about people I don't know or don't care for. All I can think about is something way too esoteric for everyday conversation. This is the Ti Si loop, by the way. I'm sure you've had experiences like this before. It's obsession. It may be a passion, but the word "passion" sounds too nice and gooey to me. The word "obsession" seems more true to my personal experience.

Interests and Obsessions

So, how do you follow the Ne? Listen and look for everything and anything that captures your attention, then follow it. Give yourself the freedom to pursue whatever minor itch you've developed. I've had an itch for computer programming for a while. I'm not sure when it first developed but there was a moment in my life when I saw one of my friends, who was going to school at the time for programming, sitting at his computer, typing all the crazy symbols that go into communicating with computers. Something slipped into my head. It was a quiet little, "Huh. That's interesting." The Ne was calling, telling me to follow it into the

On Purpose, Interests, and Obsessions

desert. It said I could one day be a programmer if I wanted. This led me to a website called Freecodecamp, and I completed the first couple of HTML exercises.

That's exploration. For several months, I worked incredibly hard on the website, going through all kinds of doubt in my head whenever I became stumped about a project. I read several books on HTML, CSS, and JavaScript. Mind you, I'm an English major and didn't have any training in the STEM fields. I had a lot of doubt and constantly wondered if I could follow through with the pursuit. Also, I'm not one of those high-IQ people who seem to love telling everyone how smart they are and how they can learn anything. I've never been tested, and I never want to be tested because I'm afraid I'd get a really low score, like 95 or something. I'd have to take myself less seriously than I already do.

Anyway, I spent every waking moment pursuing the world of programming, specifically JavaScript. The obsession had turned into a full-blown obsession that bled into my dreams. I dreamed about being inside a computer. A man was standing in front of me. He was a program that I had created, and he was smiling. He knew something. He knew that I could never leave the world of the program I had created—or something like that. I remember seeing a power button at the top right of my vision. It looked like the power button on an Xbox 360. I pressed the button to end the program and get out of the world, but nothing happened. I couldn't leave. I was stuck. The program started laughing at me because he knew I could never leave this place. I woke up the next day, thinking, 'Maybe I've been too focused on finishing the FCC's curriculum.'

I'm not trying to show you how amazing I am. I just want to show you the process of interests and obsessions, which are engines that drive the Ne. Whenever you find yourself going, "Huh. That's interesting," pursue whatever that is and see where it takes you. You don't know where it will lead. It may be a new place where you wouldn't mind living for a while.

As an INTP, you will develop many interests, and many of them you will not pursue very far. Life is short and there aren't enough hours in the day to do everything. You'll have to give up on some interests to pursue others that you deem more important or meaningful. But you have to keep listening to yourself and keep pursuing the Ne rabbit trails. Most INTPs say their Ne is their greatest source of happiness in life, and as I look over my life, I fully and completely 100% agree. If you stay comfortable in your Ti Si loop for too long, it gets depressing—like, really, really depressing. The savior, Ne, must come along and revive your being. You have to let it. You have to listen for those interests that will bring you new life and, eventually, new life to the people around you.

Circumambulation

Before I learned about circumambulation and Jung's thoughts on the phenomenon, I described my interests to my wife as a merry-go-round. It's like I'm jumping from one hobby horse to the next, repeating a cycle that I've been on for my entire life, it seems. I've never had one interest that I've stuck to. Right now, because I'm on my writing kick, I wished I had stuck with writing my entire life, but my life hasn't pulled me along that path. I jump from hobby

On Purpose, Interests, and Obsessions

horse to hobby horse, sometimes adding new horses to this merry-go-round of my life.

I didn't fall onto the religious idea of circumambulation until recently, but it perfectly describes what we're all falling into as we try to understand who we are and where we fit in the world. Circumambulation is a process. Wiki describes the phenomenon as "the act of moving around a sacred object or idol." The idea is repeated throughout almost every religion. In Hinduism, there are temples full of passageways that circle around an enshrined deity. The worshiper will go through several passageways, circling until he or she ends up in the middle of what had been circled: an idol of some sort.

In Christianity, members of the Greek Orthodox Church in Romania will circle the church three times before entering Easter Mass.

In Islam, the Kaaba is the most circumambulated structure in the world.

I'm basically summarizing the different religions on the Wikipedia page, "Circumambulation." If you wish to study the phenomenon further, you can Google the word and read about all the religious versions of circumambulation. But you should get the basic idea.

Carl Jung, the famous Swiss psychologist, believed interests in life are a circumambulatory event. You are moving around something sacred, like a potential "you" whom you could become if you kept up with the pursuit, allowing everything to die that kept you from moving forward and following through with your interests. You, as an INTP, should have interests that seem to repeat themselves throughout your life, but, unfortunately, obstacles and psychological baggage hold you back.

As I mentioned, members of the Greek Orthodox Church in Romania circle the church building three times on Easter. Each circle represents a day when Christ was dead and buried in the tomb. This version of circumambulation represents death. In the desert, the Israelites circled around for forty years until the old men, with their dead ways of thinking, died off to make way for young, fresh minds. Death is a very important process everyone must go through to meet whatever, or whoever, is waiting for us in the middle of what we are all circling.

So far, I've described the idea as only a religious event, but I believe it can be described through the lens of naturalism as well (though I'm not a naturalist). I don't think God, or the process of evolution, would give us these interests if we couldn't complete them. For instance, maybe you have an interest in mathematics that you wish to pursue, but doubt seeps in and you aren't sure if you're smart enough to start and finish that pursuit. Is it possible for you to follow through on this desire? Is it possible to have an interest in something like the pursuit of a bachelor's in mathematics if you weren't capable of obtaining the degree?

God, or the process of evolution, created you, or God created you through the process of evolution, or whatever. Would God, or the process of evolution, create a squirrel with the instinct to crack a nut it can't break? I don't think so. If a squirrel did wish to crack open a nut, but couldn't, that particular squirrel should be long dead and extinct. The squirrel's interest wouldn't be conducive to

On Purpose, Interests, and Obsessions

its survival. I believe the same thing about God. I don't think He would give me interests I wasn't capable of completing.

There are a thousand different ideas to infer from circumambulation. If you have an interest in something, if you go, "Huh. That's interesting," it means you are capable of following through with the pursuit. If you aren't capable, either there's something wrong with the process of evolution (that it created you with faulty instincts) or God has other plans.

So, why do I doubt? Why do I think back on my horrible grades in high school mathematics but have this whispering interest in pursuing higher education in the field? With the idea of circumambulation, I believe that doubt means something different. Doubt doesn't mean you can't do the thing you wish to do. It means you must change or transform into the sacred object you've been circling your entire life. Doubt means you're doing something, you have a vice or you carry psychological baggage that must die for you to move forward.

This, in its essence, is called faith. You can't be 100% sure to follow through with the process because you can't prove it wrong and you can't prove it right 100%. If someone pursues an education in mathematics and fails, what do you say to that person? "Oh, you must not have believed in yourself." The person must have carried too many vices with him and didn't believe properly. It's a pat answer. The answer could also be, "Well, maybe they had an improper interest in the field. There's something fundamentally wrong with him or her." You see, there's no real way to prove or disprove either proposition.

You have to either move forward with the doubt or not pursue the interest at all, and not do anything you wish to do for the rest of your life. Just stay in your room until the antidepressants wear off, and then you'll have to face the big question of philosophy all over again. But I believe it is to listen for those little interests to pop up and move forward from there, to let yourself become the person who can actually do the things you wish to do, whether you want to be a violinist, comic book author, fiction author, programmer, business owner, mathematics professor, gospel preacher, architect, reality TV star, documentary producer ... whatever it is that has caught your attention for whatever reason.

So, according to Jung, our interests are taking us somewhere. Where, exactly? It won't be the same for any of us, but Jung believed that our interests are circling us around our most optimal, developed selves. So, I implore you all, including myself, to look out for interests, listen for them, and pursue them. It's the Ne taking over, pulling us out of our depressed Ti Si loops, the interests that eventually snowball into obsessions.

The Process of the Pursuit

When an interest comes around and pulls you, you don't quite know what it is or what it will turn into. You are blind to it. You don't understand it fully. When I did nothing but read books on programming for six months, all I thought about was becoming a software engineer. I had ideas for games I could create, or different apps that would make the world a more efficient place. But as I pursued these interests, I began to see more of what it would mean for me to become a software engineer.

On Purpose, Interests, and Obsessions

It would eventually consume my life, giving me less time to pursue other interests. I didn't exactly give up on the idea of becoming a software engineer, but I set the idea to the side and jumped onto another hobby horse of mine. For those six months, I didn't read anything besides books on programming. I used to read all kinds of books all the time: biographies, novels, nonfiction. I have hundreds of books on shelves, a library just down the road, and more than four hundred books I haven't read on my Kindle, and my obsessive pursuit into the world of programming was making me sad that I didn't have time to read or write. I know this may sound stupid, but I didn't realize how much time learning to program would take away from my life. So, I went back to my love of reading and writing.

This happens with any interests that you or I pursue. You don't really know where the interest will bring you. You just have to follow it and then you'll know. I've heard that the process of an INTP discovering his or her interest is a lot like throwing spaghetti noodles onto a wall. I really like the example and I've thought about it a lot for myself. You have to give yourself the freedom to pursue those things that are pulling you, that you come across and go, "Hmm, that's interesting." Take the spaghetti noodle and throw it onto the wall, see if it sticks. See if it's something you want to learn more about and pursue further.

Any pursuit that you follow will change you in some way. You'll become a different person. This will be the transformation process as you circle around the sacred object, which is a potential you. It's somebody whom you could be. Every choice and interest changes the sacred object you are circumambulating. Maybe you're on your way to becoming a professor in biology, or a gospel preacher, or a hotel manager, or a writer. Or maybe you're choosing all of those things, switching back and forth from one to the other, letting your Ne go wild.

This is what Carl Jung says about the process of this circling around from interest to interest: "I began to understand that the goal of psychic development is the self. There is no linear evolution; there is only a circumambulation of the self. Uniform development exists, at most, at the beginning; later, everything points toward the centre."

A fun thing to do with interests is to combine them to make new categories. You likely know who Joe Rogan is. He's probably the biggest podcaster right now. I'm 95% sure the guy is an ENTP, and most people online agree—though people online are the furthest thing from reliable sources when it comes to MBTI typing. But the guy's Ne is off the charts, and he's successful at many different interests. Early in his life, he was a kickboxer and got into fighting. Later, he became a comedian. He has more interests than those, like hunting or sitting around with friends and smoking weed, talking about the universe and DMT.

He wasn't the greatest at his interests early on, but I think he really began to bloom when he pulled them together. He's an okay comedian, and he wasn't a very good fighter—not good enough to make it in the UFC. But he pulled those interests together and became the most successful UFC commentator as well as the most successful podcaster. He pulled his hobby horses together and created new ones. I believe that's where the real magic is, because you start to create new categories. You can do this with your own life.

On Purpose, Interests, and Obsessions

I've told you about some of my own interests, and I'm in the process of combining some of them. I'm in the middle of programming a game I hope to put on the market sometime next year. It's sort of a cyberpunk RPG. I'm hoping to combine my love of stories by programming a game, like the old Final Fantasy stuff on the Super Nintendo. So far, as I'm writing this book, I've programmed only the battle sequences, which I think will be most of the work. I'm hoping to get the game on Xbox, PlayStation, and the computer, but we'll see where I am a year from now, which will be the year 2020. My wife and I just had a kid, so that will take a chunk of my time. We'll see how it goes.

So far, my life interests have taken me all over the place: religious studies, books, computers, and stories. It seems that programming a game with an RPG storyline is starting to pull together a lot of what I've accumulated in life, but who knows? This is just an example of what circumambulating looks like.

Others and Your Interests

When you're around people who are different from you, they're going to question or make fun of you for pursuing many different things. That happens to me, especially with my family. But that's okay. This may prevent you from pursuing those things that seem to be pulling you, but you can't let it do that. I can't tell you the full reason why the people around me will make fun of me or tell me things like I need to settle down and get more focused. I'm not always sure if they have what's best for me in mind or if they're attempting to keep me from becoming something else— something that I want to be, or just something more than I am. Or if they're trying to protect me, trying to keep me from running into a wall that I can't see.

You have to give yourself permission to pursue whatever it is you wish to pursue and to keep moving forward, circling whatever it is that you're circling. Unfortunately, a big reason why people don't give themselves permission to pursue things of interest is the people around them, like friends or family. They won't fully understand what you're trying to do because you won't understand what you're trying to do, either. I'm not sure if Charles Crumb ever tried getting out of the situation he drifted into. And I'm not sure how it would go if he ever tried. I wonder what his mother would say. What would his brother say to him? Were they trying to hold him back, keep him from pursuing things? In a perfect world, his friends and family would encourage him, but, of course, the world isn't perfect and we shouldn't expect it to be.

In college, I took a course on personality types, which sent me down the rabbit hole of personalities, for both the Myers-Briggs Type Indicator and the Big Five personality test. On the Big Five, INTPs are very high in the trait "openness." We're all very high in looking at things from new perspectives. My wife is very low and doesn't have the same number of interests that I do. One thing about being very high and about trait openness is the desire to create things. You are pulled in many directions and wish to make sense of the things that are just beyond your understanding. One way to make sense of it all is through creation, which is why many INTPs spend their time writing.

In conversation, I'm not very good at holding an audience because I drift in and out of an aloof state, very unaware of the emotional needs of the people around me. So, writing seems to be the best course for many INTPs, including me. I have thoughts and ideas that have reached critical mass and that wish to present themselves into the world, but very few avenues are open for my interests and ideas. What do I do about it? What do you do about it? You have to find something, like podcasting, or starting your own YouTube channel. Today, there are many different avenues you can take to communicate your ideas with people who would find them interesting.

As you start to pursue the ideas, you must talk with the people closest to you, who are attached to you, who will be affected by you going through these changes. When I was single, I could do pretty much anything I wanted, but now that I'm married and responsible for my little girl, these conversations have to come up with my wife. Otherwise, I'll be cursed to push the rock up the hill over and over again for all eternity in a mindless, unconscious state, a form of death, suicide.

Conclusion

Because you're reading this book, you must want to learn to be more productive. This tells me that you want to get out there into the world and actually do things besides sitting in your room all day, thinking about life and its meaning (or lack thereof). You must want to move past your nihilistic tendencies. You've sat around for long enough as the walls around you have closed and you've wished for a world where you are more free. To do this, you now know that you must move beyond the certainty of things, beyond the Ti Si loop, and pursue what has caught your attention.

The process of the pursuit is a religious idea called circumambulation, in which you are turning into the self, as Carl Jung calls it. It's also called the "potential you" by other self-help people, or to self-actualize, or whatever. But in your pursuit, as you throw the spaghetti noodles onto the wall, you will begin to see the interest a lot more clearly. You will begin to know whether this is something you'd like to do. However, to prepare yourself for the journey, you must at least attempt to get the people around on your side, to make life a little bit easier for yourself and the people you care about. They won't know what you're doing because you won't, either, and that's one of the fun parts of the process.

CHAPTER 3:
ON HABITS

"As it is not one swallow or one fine day that makes a spring, so it is not one day or a short time that makes a man blessed and happy."

— Aristotle

In the first chapter, I stuck mainly to the two different cognitive functions: Ti and Ne. This chapter is dedicated to the third cognitive function of the INTP, introverted sensing. Some of the things Si desires are habits, routines, and safety. You can think of the function as memory, but it's not just memory or reviewing things again and again, but also internal sensations, like the taste and smell of things. How do you feel? Not the emotional question of how you feel, but how do you physically, empirically, feel? Are you hungry, thirsty, tired? Those kinds of things.

The good people at personalityhacker.com have an interesting metaphor to help one understand the cognitive stacks. Think of them as a family driving a vehicle. The Ti is the driver, the Ne is in the passenger seat, and then you have the Si and Fe sitting in the back, making suggestions about where to go. The poor baby, Fe, is constantly ignored. She's very emotional and underdeveloped, so we don't give her a lot of trust or attention. However, we allow our secretary, the nine-year-old girl, Si, help with navigation from time to time. She holds all the data the Ti is constantly moving around, rearranging it into something that makes more sense.

Because Si is in the third slot, as the nine-year-old girl in the back seat, we have the desire to develop helpful habits. But that's about it, just a desire. We don't really have much follow-through on the habits and routines created. You've probably tried to develop habits before, when you learned how important they are and how they are the sum total of every being. I'm constantly fighting bad habits and trying to create and enhance good ones.

One explanation as to why this is difficult is the person sitting in the passenger seat of the cognitive stack—the one second in charge, the Ne, or the exploration function. Ne and Si are the yin and yang to each other. One is sensing and one is intuitive—complete opposites. One is extroverted and one is introverted—also complete opposites. One wishes to destroy the old way of doing things no matter what, and the other wishes to hold onto the old way of doing things no matter what. So, what do you do? It's hard to know unless there's a goal. Before moving forward, we have to ask: What is the goal? What is it that you want?

Carl Rogers, the famous psychoanalyst, believed that the goal of psychology is to bring the person into their fully actualized state. How does one do this? What is the path toward actualization? He used the word "congruency" and by it, he meant something like: All the different parts of the person work in harmony with one another. In our case, this means we have to get our Si on our side. We can't keep ignoring the nine-year-old girl who wishes to control our lives and make everything as predictable and safe as possible. We have to let her do something. The best thing for her to do is to keep repeating our good habits while not stifling Ne's desire for possibilities. So, how is that done?

Aristotle on Habits

According to Aristotle, a habit is a mode of action, and the mode of the action could be either good or bad, making it either a vice or a virtue. The difference between a vice and a virtue is what moves one to act. There's a funny word called "hexis" that is discussed in Plato's *Theaetetus*. Socrates states that knowledge must be more than passive stored memory. Hexis, according to Aristotle, is moral virtue in action, and therefore, a good habit, the things we repeatedly do, must be supplemented with beneficial knowledge. Of course, knowing how to act with beneficial knowledge is called wisdom.

This is all goal-oriented information. When I say "beneficial knowledge," what does that mean without a goal in mind? It means nothing. If, say, you wanted to become an Olympic athlete in the 100-meter dash, this would create beneficial actions and non-beneficial actions, all depending on what the goal is. If there is no desired outcome, what does it matter if you want good habits? What makes a habit good if there's nothing on which to base our judgments? Of course, this is why I decided to write this chapter after writing about pursuing interests, goals, and purposes. By now hopefully you have at least something in mind, however little it may be.

Our repeated actions must avoid becoming mindless habits. This isn't the same thing as virtue. This is called "conditioning," according to the behavioralist, B. F. Skinner. Once, Skinner was lecturing to a class that, over the course of a semester, conditioned him to stand on one side of the classroom. The class schemed to smile and nod their heads while Skinner taught on one side of the classroom, and when he would walk toward the other side, the students would frown, yawn, or simply not pay attention. Eventually, unbeknownst to him, they conditioned the professor to stand on one side of the classroom. He slipped into a mindless state of action, which is the thing we are trying to avoid.

Once we have a goal and have replaced bad habits with beneficial ones, according to Aristotle, the outcome is equilibrium, otherwise known as "character." Even if the situation around us changes, we stick to our habits. For example, say we end the habit of eating sugar and somehow find ourselves in a candy store. Our character holds us back from purchasing the sugar for sale. We are in a state of equilibrium. Even if our current context calls us to perform actions that aren't beneficial, we refrain from performing those actions.

The Efficiency of Habits

What we do every day is the most important thing. We can do some math to see if this is true or not. Lately, I've been developing the habit of watching YouTube on my phone before I go to bed. I know it's not the best habit and I could replace it with something I would consider more beneficial. I'm not sure how long I watch YouTube at night, but we'll say an hour. We take that hour and multiply it by every day of the year: 365. That's easy; 365×1 hour equals 365 hours, which is a total of 15.2 days. What if we stretch that out to an entire decade? It would be 152 days of watching YouTube at night before I go to sleep.

What if we supplemented that time with something that I found was more beneficial to me, more aligned with my pursuits? Okay, I just Googled how long it takes to write a novel. Some of the websites said around 800 hours. So, 152×24= 3,648 total hours watching YouTube in a decade. If, instead, I chose to write, hypothetically, I could have written 4.56 novels instead, which in this theoretical context sounds very pleasing to me.

We use willpower when we create new habits. But what is this mysterious substance called "willpower"? Many people believe it's the thing holding them back from changing, from becoming the person they wish to be. One definition would be the energy to refrain from engaging in temptation. Another definition, stated more positively, is the energy exerted to do something. Willpower is stated in either a negative or a positive way. It's the thing you use to keep yourself from doing something you don't want to do, or the energy you use to get yourself to do something you want to do. However, to use it, you must have a will in the first place. You must be an actual person and not some mindless non-playable character going about life because that's how you were programmed. You must be a person with desires, hopes, and dreams. Then willpower comes into play.

When habits are created, it takes less willpower to follow through on whatever task. For example, try imagining every single action it takes to walk to your car, get in, and start it, and then drive away. I'm talking about every single action. Like, bend my knee, lift my foot and move it forward, set it on the ground, click the button to unlock the car, slip my hand over the handle, pull, open the door, twist my hips to slide into the driver's seat, bend down, grab the door, close it, put the key in the ignition, turn the car on, grab the seat belt, pull it over my shoulder, click it into the buckle, put my hands on the wheel, look over my shoulder, put the car in reverse ... yada-yada-yada. It's ridiculous. But all those movements, all those actions, were created through willpower at some point in your life and now getting into your car is a mesh of microhabits you don't think about because you don't have to. Willpower is depletable energy; psych tests have demonstrated this proposition more than a thousand times. This is all to say, the more habits we have, the less willpower it takes to perform beneficial actions.

The Nature of Habit

Apparently, it was researchers at MIT who discovered the three steps of a habit. I'm sure you're aware of this by now, or at least could discover the nature of a habit on your own. The three steps are: 1) cue, 2) routine, and 3) reward. It's simple enough, but I don't think understanding the nature will help you create better habits on its own; rather, interacting with the dissection of the nature of a habit will help. It's being aware of habits you want to change, and all of this is impossible if you don't have a goal in mind.

Really, if you don't have a goal in mind, no one action is better than another. You are floating around in a completely disoriented state. However, when you have goals, actions take on a more positive form. In fact, your brain knows whether you are moving toward your aims once the goals are set in place. Your brain starts

On Habits

to dump dopamine into your system, telling you, "Hey, good job. You're doing the right thing."

Now, because you know the destination, an idea your Ne came up with, your Si wants to get involved and create habits to help you get to where you want to be. You know the habits that are hindering you. For me, as I'm writing this book, it's a YouTube habit that has mindlessly crept into my life, as well as an eating-too-much-at-night habit. I do fine throughout the day, eating and everything, but lately, at night, I've been stuffing myself madly with food. The next day, I never feel as good as I'd like, especially with those carbs lingering in my digestive system throughout the night. Anyway, I'll get into dieting in another chapter.

The cue, or trigger, happens sometime between me stuffing my face after I get home from work and when I go to bed. It's really that I get bored, too, and that I'm mentally exhausted because it's the end of the day and I've just stuffed myself mindlessly with food I'm going to regret later. I sit on the couch or in my bed, and I have nothing else to do, so I open my phone and open the YouTube app. Trigger, routine. Normally, it's not hard for me to find something on YouTube that will make me laugh or that I find interesting … and voila, reward: finding something funny or interesting.

So, what habit would I rather have instead of mindlessly watching YouTube? I have hundreds of books that I want to read. Maybe instead of watching YouTube, I could open a book at the end of the day, a book that I've been wanting to read. Reading at night has always been a wonderful way to get myself to fall asleep, which has been an issue for me for the past, I don't know, decade.

So, cue, routine, reward: Those are the solidified steps to creating a habit. The knowledge of the nature of habit, though, doesn't mean anything until we actually put the information into practice. Aristotle calls this the word that we learned earlier: hexis. The nature of habit must become a virtue for us if we wish to move closer to the thing, the sacred object, the potential us, that we are currently circling.

Habits with Goals

This section has somewhat to do with the previous chapter, in which we talked about interests and goals. Creating new habits can be difficult, especially if you are trying to make consciously good habits. You must use willpower to create a habit, and willpower requires energy. One way to make the creation of habits less painful, and that costs less willpower, is to have a goal supplementing them. As you move toward whatever goal you have decided is worth pursuing, your actions become more rewarding, depending on how much you desire the outcome and how high the goal is.

Most people don't have a lack of desire or motivation. What most people lack—and this includes me and almost all INTPs everywhere—is clarity. You've probably heard about the marshmallow study. This was a recent study that clarified why some kids delay gratification. The researchers found that affluent backgrounds help children with the marshmallow study. However, during the study, one child passed the marshmallow test and then did one thing different from the rest of the kids. Before the test started, he said to himself, "When I get the other marshmallow,

On Habits

I'll eat them both at the same time." He was the only child to last the full fifteen minutes, and when the marshmallow came, he grabbed both of them and shoved them into his mouth.

If the children were asked whether they desired both marshmallows, they would've said yes. Of course, they would've said yes, or else they wouldn't have eaten the first marshmallow. But it was this one child who actually provided a clear statement of what he was going to do when he had both marshmallows. He was able to withstand the fifteen minutes with the marshmallow sitting in front of him on the table.

This is a good example of a child using willpower to keep himself from gratification now so that he could have more gratification later. He goes back to the entire principle I'm trying to get to in this book. The example of the child is a microcosm of what I'm trying to explain, and of what I'm trying to understand for myself. The child had discipline for fifteen minutes and got double the portion of marshmallows as all the other kids. If you extrapolate that principle to all of life, we get more as an outcome.

INTPs—including most people—don't necessarily want marshmallows as a goal. In fact, I'm trying to stay away from them because of what sugar does to me. What I really want is the freedom to pursue my interests. Really, I want the freedom to do what I want. But, unfortunately, life doesn't just hand me freedom as a gift. I think I've lived a lot of my life thinking that way, at least unconsciously. If life did work that way, why were so many people around me held captive by their own vices? I want to put myself on a set of habits that will bring the most freedom. And the best way I've found to establish a habit inside the stacks of scientific and self-help literature is to have clarified goals holding the beneficial actions together.

There were times when I'd been the most in-shape in my life, or when I had in-shape goals. I used to be in the military—the U.S. Army, specifically—and whenever I had a PT test coming up, I would train for it. Right now, I can't do nearly as many push-ups or sit-ups, or run as fast for two miles. After work, it was like clockwork. I would go home, walk to the gym, and exercise, with the goal of the PT test in mind. A few years ago, I signed up for a half marathon because I know it would give me the motivation to run more. And it worked. I ran more training for that half marathon than I had in my entire life. Habits are what we want to help us pursue whatever we find worth pursuing, and goals help us hold those habits together and make doing them easier.

Breaking Habits

Do you want to know how difficult it is to break a habit? I'll tell you. It's exactly how difficult as you think it is. I'm not saying it's as difficult as you make it. I'm talking objective here. Ask yourself about the habit you want to replace and the new one you wish you had. How hard do you think it will be to replace? Really think about it. It's going to be that hard. Replacing habits isn't easy and replacing some may be the hardest thing you ever do in your life. I say this because I believe it's important to be honest with ourselves about how difficult it is to go against decade-old, established, unbeneficial, repeated actions. Whenever I have gone against a habit, thinking it will be easy, I have fallen on my face or fallen into a habit even worse than the previous one. I want to stop eating ice cream altogether. Three days from now, you'll find me in a dark corner in my house with a suicidal-sized bowl of ice cream.

There's no easy way to break habits. Eventually, willpower must be involved. Then again, maybe you've found a way to make the breaking and creation of habits easy. However, I doubt it, and I haven't discovered the fix-it-all solution to habits yet. You're going to have to become aware of your cues, routines, and rewards and then flip them around to create better and more productive days. There's no way around it. Well, I cringe a little saying that there's no way around it because maybe there is. But I have yet to find it.

You must pay attention to cues. What happens before you start a bad habit? For me and my bad habit of coming home and stuffing my face with food in the pantry, the cue strikes when I get home from work. I'm tired and my willpower is low. Most importantly, the strongest cue of all, I'm hungry. I just start mindlessly eating food out of the pantry like a zombie over a fresh cadaver. What happened?

Now that we have the bad habit in mind, how do we break it? Well, I didn't really name the section of this chapter very well because we aren't necessarily breaking habits as much as we are replacing them. Again, I haven't found a way to simply break a habit without replacing the routine following the cue.

So, this is what I've been doing. I've been listening to something I find interesting on my iPhone—a podcast, an audiobook, or something that has caught my attention on YouTube while playing Tetris, specifically, the Tetris Blitz app on iPhone. I do this after I have eaten my set amount for the night, and I see how I feel after playing one round of Tetris. Normally, one round takes me about ten to fifteen minutes when I start on level one. I do this because I read a study about how Tetris can help victims of PTSD. It helps take up the visual space in the mind so they aren't triggered by whatever is causing the panic attacks to happen. It also helps with food cravings. Plus, I enjoy a few rounds of Tetris. https://www.scientificamerican.com/article/tetris-shown-to-lessen-ptsd-and-flashbacks/

What happens when you mess up? Honestly, I think this is where INTPs shine better than most other types. I think INTPs are generally good at breaking habits when they've spotted something they wish to change, because we have an analytical detachment whenever a mistake occurs. I've heard (though I can't find on the internet where I read this, so take it with a grain of salt) that INTPs are the most likely type to pick up the habit of smoking but also the most likely type to quit the habit. One reason why I think INTPs quit habits possibly more easily than other types do is that they aren't as hard on themselves when they mess up. When one is trying to create better habits, messing up is an inevitable part of the process.

I talked to some friends about their bad habits and asked whether they have tried to break them and create new ones. People are surprisingly hard on themselves, which I've never understood. I have yet to see whether the anger or the upset-ness helps one quit or change a habit. I don't think it does.

One technique that helps when and where we mess up is to think, 'Well, that's some good data,' and then later turn that data into comprehensible information. What happened? What's the good data? Well, I got home and I was tired and hungry, so I went straight to the pantry. Well, tomorrow, I'm going to try and substitute a new habit for that one—a new habit that I find more beneficial to me. I'm going to start playing Tetris on my phone after I eat what I have set out for myself. And the next day, I mess up again. Well, maybe I should just get rid of all the bad food in the pantry. I've thought about this, but I'll have to have a conversation with my wife about that. So far, though, the Tetris thing has been working for me and I enjoy it.

Anyway, when you mess up, just think to yourself, 'Well, that's good data.' Analyze it until it becomes comprehensible information. When you make a mistake, collect the good data (Ne), and then analyze it (Ti and Si), and then come up with a new strategy (Ne). If that new strategy works, keep repeating (Si). And repeat it for how long?

Time and New Habits

For a while, the word on the street was that it took twenty-one days for a habit to solidify. But this isn't exactly true. The idea originated from a study by Dr. Maltz, the author of the famous book *Psycho-Cybernetics*. He was a plastic surgeon in the 1950s who noticed a pattern with his patients in terms of how long it took them to get used to their new facial reconstructions.

In a journal, he wrote, "These, and many other commonly observed phenomena tend to show that it requires a minimum of about 21 days for an old mental image to dissolve and a new one to jell." And ever since, people have thought that it takes twenty-one days to create a habit. Zig Ziglar, Tony Robbins, Jim Rohn,

Brian Tracy, and many more have contributed to the idea that it takes twenty-one days to make a habit. Unfortunately, though there is a nugget of truth to it, twenty-one days isn't the full story of habit creation. In fact, if we look back at the original source, Dr. Maltz doesn't exactly say it takes twenty-one days; rather, he said "that it requires a minimum of twenty-one days," which is more on target than saying twenty-one days outright.

Since then, a new famous study has come to town and people are starting to change the time frame of habit creation. https://onlinelibrary.wiley.com/doi/abs/10.1002/ejsp.674

Ninety-six people participated in the study. It says, "The time it took participants to reach 95% of their asymptote of automaticity ranged from 18 to 254 days." What does that mean? Basically, that Dr. Maltz was kind of right, that it can take twenty-one days for a habit to solidify, but it could also take eighteen days, the shortest time in the study, or it could take 254 days. I think to myself, 'What? I really hope it doesn't take 254 days for me to create a habit.'

Now, quoting from the famous habit study, people are spreading new information on the street, and it's not eighteen to 254 days, but sixty-six days to create a habit. Sixty-six was the average of all the participants in the study, so it will most likely take you—and me—sixty-six days to create a repeated automated action that will take much less willpower and make our days more efficient. Personally, I found that if I track a habit and stay with it for about a month, that's normally how long it takes for the repeated action to become basically automatic.

On Habits

Habit creation takes several stages. Hal Elrod, in his book *The Miracle Morning*, discusses the stages of a new habit. I got some of my ideas from him. The first week is called the infatuation stage. I'm normally really excited about some routine I wish to implement, so for the first week I do well and execute the new habit with enthusiasm. For about the next three weeks after the first, my enthusiasm abates until the habit is carried over into the span of a month. Once I move past the four-week mark, I am no longer enthusiastic about the habit but ... however ... but ... here's the thing ... the new repeated action becomes easier.

I try to carry over my enthusiasm for as long as I can, but after one week, whatever habit I'm trying to create becomes dull and boring, and I hate it. I think, as an INTP, that coming up with ideas for new habits can be fun. Our Ne likes to come up with new ideas but, unfortunately, our Ne isn't the same function that helps us stick to the new habit; rather, it's the opposite function, Si.

Like I said before, because our Si is underdeveloped, learning to stick to a new habit can be quite difficult. I think it's difficult for anyone. My wife, for example, leads with Si, but because she leads with Si, she also suppresses Ne. Therefore, it's almost impossible for her to come up with a new idea for a routine because she's very trapped inside her routine world. She also has a difficult time creating new habits, like anyone else, but for different reasons. Specifically, I think that INTPs have a good cognitive stack to help us both create and stick to new habits, though that doesn't mean creating a new habit will be easy.

Still, there are some things that will help.

Tracking Habits

There is some irony to the idea of tracking a habit. Tracking habits itself is a habit, one that will be very useful if you follow through on the habit of tracking habits. Tracking habits has been difficult for me. I know that a big reason why we're supposed to track habits is to help us analyze the information later, to help us see what is either helping or hurting. However, the very act of tracking a habit actually helps keep you, and me, consistent with whatever habit we're trying to create.

There are many ways to track habits. You can get as complicated as you want with any habit tracking system. You can have an Excel sheet with all kinds of numbers and colors for the cells, with thousands of metrics and a section for journaling about how a particular habit went that particular day. It can become very overwhelming at first, so I suggest starting small and simple.

Jerry Seinfeld, when he was an up-and-coming comic, would keep a calendar on the wall. He wanted to write a joke a day, so on the calendar, he would check the day if he wrote a joke during it. I really like this strategy because it's simple and keeps you on track. You can visually look at your progress by staring at a calendar.

When tracking habits, initially you don't want to focus on the efficiency and effectiveness of whatever habit tracking system you use. Rather, you want to seek a system that doesn't take a lot of work, that you can keep repeating. You want a habit tracking system that you will actually use. I've used about a dozen things in the past.

On Habits

One system that I really liked was an app called Habitica. It's an RPG game in which you have an avatar that starts at level one. You create habits for yourself and a to-do list for the day. As you complete the to-do list and complete your daily habits, you get experience points and level up your avatar. It was fun, but after three months, I had all the weapons and gear for my rogue character. The game lost a lot of its flair.

Right now, I use an app called Good Habits. It's basically a calendar for any habit that I want to track. It's the very same concept that Jerry Seinfeld used back in the day. However, this isn't the 1970s. We have apps for everything. If I complete the habit for that day, I simply open the app and tap the date to show that I completed the habit. That's all there is to it. I don't journal about it or anything. It would probably help me if I journaled my habits but, honestly, I don't think I would keep up with journaling. I've tried it before. For some reason, it just didn't stick. And honestly, I don't want to journal. I'd rather do something else.

The act of tracking a habit helps you stick with that habit, but it also gives you good data about why a habit is either working or not. Later, you can review your tracked habits, using the Ti and Si functions. Once you start analyzing and figuring out what went wrong, you can think of new solutions using your Ne function. But, remember, if you haven't been tracking habits, it's important right now for you to start the habit of tracking habits. Don't use the technology that you find interesting and cool; use technology that you will actually use. Using a method that you will repeat is more important than getting the latest technology.

Think Big with Small Steps

I mostly hate banks. In any given town or city, they are the biggest buildings. They provide the service of being responsible for the money of others. Then they lend out the money with the insane concept of interest attached to it. The interest they charge consists of little percentages, but this is the thing with percentages: what they get back compounds. And it blows my mind whenever I think about it. Banks are masters at making small numbers grow. They put up percentages like 12%, which seems harmless at first, but over time 12% interest can become larger than the loan that started it all.

More than any other institution, banks understand the power of small percentages, and they make numbers grow like crazy. But it's the small, incremental increases that make all the difference, and not just with banks but with improving our lives. It's the best way to think about habits—as incremental progress. Previously, I tried changing my entire life in a day. I wrote down everything I wanted to change and followed through with the changes for a few days but burned out. I don't want to advise you to not strive to change yourself in one day. I don't like closing that option for me or for you. However, I still haven't been able to find a way around the power of small, incremental changes.

Think of it this way. If you improved yourself 1% every single day for a year, in whatever category you wanted to improve, how good would you be? Tomorrow, you would be 101% of whatever you were today. The next day, if you improved by 1%, it would be 102.01 and the next day 103.0301. Not very exciting, and not a lot of change. But the thing with percentages and incremental

On Habits

increases is that they get out of control down the road. In a year, after 365 days of increasing everything by 1%, you become 3740.934% more than when you started the year. Another way to put it is this: 37.40934 times more than you started the year. Two years, 1413.453 times more; five years, 7624050767% or 76240507.67 times more. I'm not able to wrap my head around these percentages, but you should get the point.

This is why banks are the biggest, nicest buildings in any given city and why they pop up everywhere. They think in incremental gains. However, it's very difficult to think this way, which is why it's difficult to keep up with habits. The nature of increases by percentages has a hockey-stick-like nature. You start and put in the effort for a week or two and you see close to no change in your life. Nothing seems different, no apparent changes reveal themselves to you, and it's a little discouraging. You don't start seeing changes until sometime down the road, when the habits start to return those incremental changes.

The nature of increasing through compound interest is also why banks are able to suck people in. We can't see as far down the road as their Excel sheets do, and people don't really start owing the bank money until a year or five later. That's when people start paying only interest—or, really, that's when people are giving their money only to the bank and not to their loan. They're just handing money to the bank so the institution can keep up with all the nice things in the building, paying for the electricity, vacations, and the employee vehicles in the parking lot.

But enough about banks. Let's see this idea in action in another way. Pat Riley was the coach of the Los Angeles Lakers in 1987. The year before, they were supposed to win the NBA championship, but they fell short in the Western Conference Finals and lost to the Houston Rockets. The next year, Pat Riley came up with an idea. He wanted to implement the principle of incremental increases. Riley had all the players choose for themselves which areas they would improve by 1%. One player chose rebounds. So, if he was averaging, say, five rebounds a game, this year he would strive for 5.05 rebounds. Later that year, in 1987, the Lakers went on to win the NBA Finals.

It's not a difficult concept to grasp, but it's a difficult concept to put into practice. You don't really see the rewards of becoming better until later down the road. This is the reason why people have a hard time following through on incremental increases and why people fall prey to the bank's horrible service of loans. The rewards, or damages, aren't seen until far down the road.

CHAPTER 4:
ON ENERGY MANAGEMENT, PART 1

"In order for man to succeed in life, God provided him with two means, education and physical activity. Not separately, one for the soul and the other for the body, but for the two together. With these two means, man can attain perfection."

—Plato

Energy > Time

If you were going to read only one section of this book, I would have you read this one and the next. I find the subject of energy management to be important enough for the INTP that I have provided a "part one" chapter and a "part two" chapter. The chapter on habits was necessary because how are you going to start the habit of energy management without at least pondering the importance of habits? Writing the first two chapters, it seemed as though I was dealing with my own nihilism and the nihilism that seems to hold many INTPs captive. All that stuff is important, but only to get you to the idea of energy management (which, I find, is more important for the INTP than time management).

But hear me out. Other types will probably disagree with me, and rightly so. A lot of the advice I was given during school, as I tried to learn how to survive college, was about time management skills. Time management skills are important, and I'll get into that in the last chapter on how an INTP can plan their day—or, at least, attempt to plan their day. But, for the INTP, it is more important to manage energy than it is to manage time.

With the whole theme of freedom and discipline, this is the area of discipline on which we ADHD folks need to focus. Once, I subscribed to a podcast for people with ADHD. I was never formally diagnosed as a person with ADHD, but I've read many books and articles and listened to YouTube videos on the subject, and many of them have helped me tremendously. One piece of advice that I got from a self-professed ADHD entrepreneur was to schedule your day, minute by minute.

I was in school and I followed the technique to a T. For the next two days, I completely killed my school projects. I wrote down exactly what I was going to do that day, and then I did it. It was amazing. I thought that I'd figured out my scheduling problem with this one simple technique. Unfortunately, though, after two days, I felt stifled and claustrophobic because of my extremely precise schedule. I couldn't handle it. The next day, I rebelled against the schedule and did absolutely nothing.

Scheduling my day, I've tried thousands of techniques—honestly, about a dozen or two. I've never been able to figure it out because I hate being locked in. I hate looking at a piece of paper and seeing that this is exactly what I'm going to do today, like a

On Energy Management, Part 1

program or some mindless being, moving from one task to the next.

Using MBTI talk, for INTPs, Ne wants possibilities. Ne is always fighting against being locked in, which makes it difficult to follow a piece of paper—or whatever thing you choose—that says exactly what you will do for the day. The Ne has to shut down and not be a part of the day's process. Sure, it may be a part of the scheduling process, in which you sit down and think to yourself, 'Hmm. I wonder what I can do today?' But that's it. Once you get into the schedule and start moving from one task to the other, our Ne has to shut up, be quiet, and just mindlessly follow the schedule you created earlier.

However, in the long run, this way of planning your day isn't helpful. There's a better way to do it. This is why energy management is more important than time management. Energy management feeds the Ne. The more energy you have, the more you can do in a day, while time management makes use of your energy more efficiently. Time management is possible, but a little difficult, which I'll get into in another chapter. For now, let's talk about energy management and think about how it increases what you can <u>actually</u> do.

This all goes back to the concept of freedom and discipline. The more disciplined we are with our time management, the more efficiently we can get stuff done. Also, the more disciplined we are with energy management, the more we can actually do. This is what's so fun about energy management. When you manage your energy, you really don't know what you can do in a day, and that's a lot more fascinating for the Ne. I do believe that time management is important, but not as important as energy management. I'll get into time management in the last chapter of this book. However, we just finished a chapter about the creation of habits, so we need to focus on what habits we want.

Believe me, when you start managing your energy and gaining more of it, you are going to want to explore new ideas and concepts. You'll start to think to yourself, 'What if?' And then you will actually pursue the question because you will be confident with the oversized energy tank you are carrying. You won't have to force yourself—well, maybe a little. But you will be confident because you will have the energy, which is all the Ne really needs to explore new concepts.

The Nature of Ne

Everywhere I look for development as an INTP, I get the same answer. And now, because I've delved into the concept of Ne in my own life, I have the same conclusion. That is, for the INTP to develop, they must grow their Ne function. They must actually pursue things and stop sitting around, ruminating over the same thing in an endless cycle—the deadly Ti Si loop. INTPs who express content and happiness with their lives gain it through the Ne process. Any information I have ever truly explored, I've never regretted, even if it led to a dead end. Every book that I decided to read and finish, I've not regretted. Going through college, getting a degree in English literature (even though I've never gotten a job specifically for my degree), I don't regret. Here's a very upvoted Quora answer to the question, "How can I develop my extroverted intuition since I am [an] INTP?": https://www.quora.com/How-can-I-develop-my-extraverted-

On Energy Management, Part 1

intuition-since-I-am-INTP. And here's another very uploaded comment on Reddit: https://www.reddit.com/r/INTP/comments/46ymk4/the_key_to_personal_growth_for_an_intp_is/

I'm saying all this because, for the INTP, Ne is the way to go. I also vouch for the importance of Ne. So, why write all this stuff in a chapter about energy management? Well, Ne is a very, very energetic function. It's very centered around the neurotransmitter dopamine. Dopamine is a reward neurotransmitter but it's also a neurotransmitter that motivates pursuit. Personality types that lead with Ne, like ENTP and ENFP, are known to have manic temperaments, a form of mania—either a small hypo-case of mania or full-on hyper-mania. And mania is a great explanation for what Ne truly is.

Doc from the movie *Back to the Future* is a true ENTP. There is something insane about him, and I find that same insanity in most, if not all, ENTPs. Too many ideas are going through their heads at the same time and they can't do enough about it. They can't move fast enough, or they can't talk fast enough, or they can't get to the place where they want to be fast enough. Everything is go, go, go. This is the bad side of mania—or, in MBTI language, this is way too much Ne, which shouldn't be a problem for the INTP. This is an ENTP, ENFP issue, and also an issue of mania. Too much dopamine is running through your system, and you want to do so many things at once that you actually get nothing done at all.

Fortunately for INTPs, we have more stick-to-it-ness than ENTPs, who rush from one thing to the next almost too quickly. ENTPs could learn from INTPs, as their Ti is their growth function.

However, on the flipside, INTPs can learn a great deal from ENTPs and ENFPs. Below the Ti function, there's this energetic, insane, manic, Ne function that wants to do way too many things all at the same time. Naturally, our tertiary Si will keep the Ne from getting out of control. We just have to fall back on our natural tendencies with respect to the Ti Si loop, which will naturally refine any new concept into our Si database.

I hope I'm not scaring you away from exercising your Ne function. It won't manifest itself in the same way as it will for ENTPs. It's going to be a lot more careful and thought out. I mean, that's what we INTPs do. We think all the time, almost too much. We need to allow the dopaminergic Ne to take control, to bring us out of the pursuit of absolute certainty and into the pursuit of new ideas.

We allow the Ne function to take control, and it searches for possibilities and "what if?" questions. However, for the INTP, this is very hard to do if you have little or no energy. When we're tired, we simply fall back into a vegetative state, reviewing concepts over and over in our heads, making sure they're correct. We don't have the natural manic temperaments of ENTP or ENFP types. So, we need more energy to help us supplement our Ne function. How do we do that? How do we get the energy for Ne growth? Fortunately, there are plenty of strategies for increasing our energy tanks.

The Energy Matrix

On Energy Management, Part 1

As discussed in the first chapter, what you put into energy management is what you get out of it. The more disciplined you are with your energy, the freer you'll be to pursue new ideas.

First, I have to admit that a lot of the ideas I'm putting forth in this little book aren't my own but, rather, are a synthesis of ideas. I can't find where I found this idea about an energy matrix. It wasn't an energy matrix to start with, but an energy formula. I was listening to a podcast and the person being interviewed talked about a formula for creating more energy. I really liked the idea. For some reason, it never left me, and I still use it today. The gentleman in the podcast said that the idea was a formula, but I changed it into a matrix to make it more visual for myself; plus, *The Matrix* is my favorite movie. So, there you go. The gentleman's idea was: exercise + diet + sleep + meditation = energy. That was basically it. I never wrote it down, but I thought about the idea a lot and eventually changed the formula into a matrix. Here's an example of the energy matrix without any of the variables being measured.

The Productive INTP

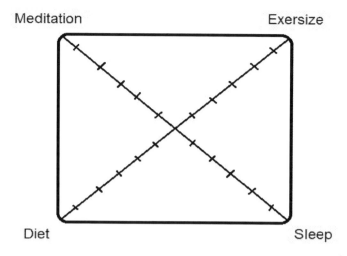

If I had to judge myself right now and how I felt, it would be something like this.

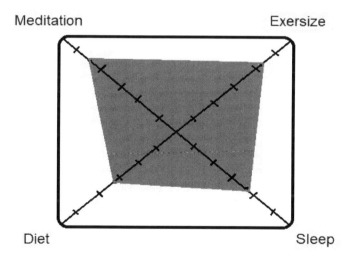

It should be somewhat intuitive. Each section of the matrix represents the potential energy that I could have, or the energy goals I have for each area. I didn't get a full eight hours of sleep

On Energy Management, Part 1

last night; instead, I got six-and-a-half. For the last couple of nights, I've been getting seven hours of sleep; one night of only six hours of sleep isn't so bad, but it's also not where I could be. Meditation—I get a break at work for an hour, and every day at work, I've been meditating for twenty minutes. I've been able to keep up with a habit pretty well.

For exercise, I don't have very high goals. I'm not looking to run a marathon or anything. I go for a run or jump on a treadmill for about twenty to thirty minutes. I normally don't end my runs before I reach three miles. So, my energy for the day is good—not where it could be, but good. I'm confident that I can sit down in front of the computer and write for a very long time and pursue this idea that's been bothering me: How can an INTP be productive?

I got the idea for the matrix from an old Pokédex magazine I had for Pokémon Red and Blue. At the back of the book, there was a Pokédex with all the different Pokémon, and a matrix representing each of the Pokémon strengths in the shape of a pentagon.

I'm not sure why I shared that but if you're an INTP under the age of thirty-five, I'm 98% sure you've played Pokémon, so you might find it interesting. The image of the Pokémon's strengths matrix is very nostalgic for me. I spent hours flipping through the magazine, learning about the game of Pokémon as much as I could. The magazine's binding eventually fell apart and I had to throw it away.

Anyway, as for the energy matrix, you can figure out your own energy level right now. What have you been eating? Fast food?

Sugar? If so, it's probably pretty low. What is your sleep schedule? Going to sleep late? Getting less than eight hours? Getting less than six hours? Your sleep may be pretty low. What about meditation? You don't meditate? That's fine. What about running? Do you exercise? Do you lift? That's also probably pretty low.

It's no wonder, then, that you feel bad all the time and don't have enough energy to pursue your interests. Hopefully, I'm wrong about all my assumptions, but if I'm not, keep reading. This concept of energy is hands-down the number-one thing you have to work on. In the previous chapter, we talked about habits. I suggest using everything you know about habit creation to create better habits for more energy. Otherwise, the Ti Si loop will eventually take over, along with all that nihilistic depression waiting at the door. You'll have no energy to supply the Ne, and you'll be stuck in the vicious cycle that leads to seeing no meaning in anything.

Now, for the rest of the next two chapters, I'm going to take a deep dive into the matrix, digging into each of the variables that create energy: meditation, exercise, diet, sleep, and anything else that would add to your overall energy tank.

The Religion of Diets

It's very difficult to talk about diets. In the past, people ate mainly from their immediate environment. You ate what the ground or the trees grew. I think people were still uptight about what you could or couldn't eat, but people from a certain area of the world just stuck to their environment and that ended the discussion.

On Energy Management, Part 1

Nowadays, food is at our disposal from all over the world. I drive a few blocks from my house, and there's a burger joint selling good ol' American food. Next to it is a Mexican restaurant, and just across town is an Asian Buffet, an Indian place, a Mediterranean place, and all sorts of food places from around the world.

Talking about what's good for you and what's not is an extremely heated conversation. For some reason, and I don't quite know why, morality is the basis of food. Food seems to be a focal point in every religion. Jews have their kosher food, while Muslims have the Halal, which states what they can and can't eat. In Christianity, unleavened bread and fruit of the vine are sacraments that represent Christ's body. In the book of Genesis, the knowledge of morality came from fruit. I know that those are mostly Abrahamic religions, but you can find food representing morality in other religions too.

But we don't have to look at religions. We can just watch people have disagreements over food and see their smugness and vicious attacks again each other, which seem to go beyond reason. There isn't a reasonable discussion of diets, but a vitriolic, self-righteous, indignant rapture on all sides. This is especially true of vegans.

Diets are still mysterious things, and I believe this goes for everyone, including self-professed diet gurus. Everyone has an opinion about them, an insane reasoning connecting one insane premise to another, creating an insane concoction. This morning, a friend of mine said this on a Facebook post:

"Carbohydrates are used as the first source of energy. When there are no carbs left in your liver or muscles, it resorts to using fat or protein as fuel ... your body turns fats or proteins into glucose to keep you functioning ... this, in turn, will leave your body..." and yada-yada-yada.

Everyone has a theory about diets. "When the ketogenesis and triglycerides curtail the elliptical's traverse over the polysaline's lubricant..." What the crap? What's even being said? I'm not trying to deter you from attempting to understand how food works in the body. I've read my own literature and attempted an understanding, but I see the same thing happening. Everyone has these big words to explain why their diet is the correct one and why all others are wrong.

About a decade ago, everyone was making a big deal about starches—specifically, potatoes. It came from the Atkins diet and its religious take on staying away from these poor, sad, little spuds. Now, there's this new all-in-one diet called the potato diet, which dismisses all the scientific research. And some people do really well on it. I'm mostly Irish. For a while, my ancestors lived off the potato and they seem to do quite well on a diet high in starches. Now everyone's making a big deal about gluten.

Honestly, I'm not here to give you the answer about diets. I have my own answers, with their own scientific studies, that prove themselves right and prove all other diets wrong. I'm still trying to figure out the world of dieting. Recently, I went through a potato phase, in which I tried to eat a potato diet, but I felt horrible. I wanted to exercise after work, but I was so weak, I had a difficult time walking to my car. My hands were shaking. I didn't feel good.

So, before I tell you what foods I find to be the most helpful when it comes to energy, you need to give yourself the freedom to try different diets. And be honest with yourself about whether a diet is working or not. I'm not talking about diets that help you lose weight. I'm talking about diets that help you focus and that give you energy throughout the day.

Energy and Food

Many INTPs are diagnosed as ADHD—or, like me, they diagnose themselves as such. I haven't really diagnosed myself as ADHD, but I do use a lot of the tools and techniques taught to kids with the diagnosis. One of those techniques is dieting. For some reason, people with ADHD seem to have food sensitivities. Some food makes them go haywire, while other types of food seem to help them. In college, before I even knew about the MBTI, I read several books on ADHD and listened to podcasts about what to do about it. One thing that came up over and over was staying away from particular foods and eating other particular foods.

Now, I believe that ADHD is more of a personality temperament than a disorder. In the modern age, I believe the way we have constructed the system of our schooling is creating the diagnosis. Not that we have brain dysfunctions or frontal lobe impairment, which is generally the explanation for why people with ADHD are the way they are. They don't have the executive faculty to help themselves make decisions or have a sense of time like other SJ types. Anyway, the modern public system sucks and personality types that have a difficult time with it are marked as disorders. However, there's something to be said about dieting as an INTP. I don't want to go on a rant about the public system. That's for a completely different book.

The first thing to eliminate from your diet is sugar. Stay away from sugar, especially today's laboratory-invented, high-fructose corn syrup, otherwise known as HFCS. That stuff literally kills the brain, and, as an INTP, your brain should be your most treasured asset. Study after study has shown that sugar damages the brain. I'll mention one. Basically, the researchers fed a controlled rat the typical American diet of fat and sugar. The normal rat—the one fed normal rat food, whatever that is—was put into a vat of water and found his way to the stump in five seconds. The second rat—the one fed the American diet—wasn't able to find the stump. The study concluded that the rat's brain had been damaged by the fat and sugar from the American diet.

Sugar impairs the brain and, over a period of time, can cause the brain to atrophy and shrink. It's associated with cancer, Parkinson's disease, Alzheimer's, and other brain-related diseases. There is nothing good about sugar except the moment when it touches your tongue. After that, sugar sucks and is killing your brain. Yes, it's also making you fatter. However, this book isn't about losing weight. As a principle, in terms of productivity, sugar sucks and takes away the freedom of your interests. Either you can choose the pleasure of it now, and the captivity of it later, or you can stay away from the drug (yes, it is a drug) and move forward with a healthy brain.

Okay, so far, sugar sucks. The next thing to remember about dieting and ADHD is that carbs kill. Sugar sucks and carbs kill. David Perlmutter's book, *Brain Grain*, revolves around the destruction of a single food type: carbohydrates. Honestly, I'm not all that concerned with good complex carbs. I do really like his book, and his principles for dieting seem to work really well for me. He's part of the low-carb, high-fat and high-protein trend circulating around the world of diets now; I would also consider myself a part of that. However, I've seen other people do well with other diets.

Several times, he quotes one study of indigenous people in Alaska, who eat a high-fat diet, specifically, whale fat. In that area of the world, the indigenous people have the lowest rate of heart disease. But, as I said before, I don't really have a huge problem with carbohydrates. Many people seem to do really well with them. I wouldn't have tried the potato diet if I hadn't thought that there was something to it. Sugar is really the biggest thing to stay away from.

Protein and fat are the way to go. By themselves, carbs cause a lot of oxidative stress on the body. The cells in your body start to oxidate and they get overwhelmed. If the damage gets out of control, the cells start going all nihilistic and self-destruct, spreading inflammation everywhere. It also causes brain fog. One way to prevent this process from happening, or at least from getting out of control, is by eating fat and protein.

Another thing to think about is blood sugar. When you eat straight-up sugar, the sugar level in your blood spikes, which causes brain fog and fatigue. You aren't going to get anything productive done with brain fog and fatigue, and if you get blood sugar spikes, you also get sugar dips. Both of these aren't good for focus or stress. One way to prevent the spikes and dips from occurring is to consume a decent portion of fat and protein. They keep the oxidation process at bay, along with all the inflammation that goes along with it.

I think the world is rediscovering the fabulousness of fat. It's no secret that the world is becoming more distrustful of institutions, like the government. As a consequence, we are starting to rediscover a lot of things, like how bad sugar really is. I know I've already harped on the issue, but if you want more information about the substance, watch the documentary *Fed Up*. It goes over the history of grain—specifically, corn—in the American market. We need to sell a lot of corn because that's what America produces; they figured out that one way to sell more corn was to pay a bunch of scientists to perform alchemy on corn and turn it into HFCS, and then to create a food pyramid with the products that America mass produced at the time, like grains and wheat.

Anyway, if there's one thing all dieters can agree with, it's to stay away from sugar. However, consuming a high quantity of fat is still a very controversial idea in some diet circles.

This might be an overly simplistic way of looking at fat, but the brain is mostly fat, approximately 60%. Now take a wild guess as to what substance has the highest amount of DHA fat. It's breast milk. Studies show that kids who breastfed longer have higher IQs than their peers. Now try to make sense of all that while holding onto the idea that fat isn't good for you. I hope you're convinced because I'm about to get serious about this topic.

I'm not writing a book on diets. I'm not here to convince you which diet is the best for you. If you aren't sure, try different diets and ignore all the zealots, with all their professions of faith in their particular tribes. My own mother preaches to me when she sees me drinking my bulletproof coffee in the morning. She eats mainly a plant diet and it really works for her. However, I can go a long time without eating when I consume a lot of fat and protein, and I have constant energy throughout the day, with no spikes or dips in energy.

As an experiment, try bulletproof coffee in the morning for a few days. Have only that for breakfast. If you don't know what bulletproof coffee is, you can give it a quick Google search. My mother calls it butter coffee. It's basically coconut oil, grass-fed butter, and whipping cream stirred in a cup of coffee.

A word of caution about indigestion: If you go the low-carb route, find a way to consume some fiber. I've been eating a lot of beans, though David Perlmutter says that beans are the devil. However, my bowels thank me when I've had a healthy amount of fiber. I have Dr. Perlmutter's cookbook, but if I eat only what's in there, the food doesn't come out the other end very nicely.

I hope I've proven my point. Try stuff. Get out there and be honest about what helps you and what doesn't. Out of the four things on the energy matrix, food is the only thing that doesn't require more of your time. Sleep requires more time, and so does meditating and exercising, but eating … You gotta eat, even if it's bad stuff. But since you gotta eat, eat something that will help you and not hinder you. Eat something that will give you more freedom and energy.

Sleep and Energy

Sleep helps clear your mind. Wow. What a profound statement … *clears throat* Sorry. Yes, but I'm here seeking an answer to the questions, "Why does sleep have this restorative function? Why does brain fog go away during sleep?" The brain is the powerhouse of the body. It uses about a quarter of the body's energy supply. This means that the brain will consume about 25% of the energy from the food you eat, which is another reason to eat well.

When the brain consumes and uses the energy from the food you eat, a problem occurs. It produces waste that sits around in our dome. Guess what this waste just sitting around in our brain is causing? Brain fog. If you know anything about anatomy, you know that the purpose of the lymphatic system is to get rid of all the abandoned waste throughout the body. But here's the problem: There are no lymphatic vessels in the brain. Whoa ... So, how does all the waste get out of our heads? That's a good question.

Basically, there's this weird fluid called cerebrospinal fluid (CSF) that flushes through the brain during sleep. The brain performs this washing job only during sleep. At all other times of the day, the brain is a working powerhouse managing every activity of the body, from conscious to unconscious actions. As we get less and less sleep, the fogginess in the brain builds up and everything becomes murkier.

Joe Rogan once hosted, on his podcast, a neurologist named Matthew Walker. He talked about a study performed in Wyoming with high school kids. They decided to change the start times for schools from 7:35 am to 8:55 am. That year, there were 70% fewer reports of car crashes than the following year. In the workplace, underslept employees—who, according to Matthew Walker, are those people who get less than eight hours of sleep—

On Energy Management, Part 1

will take on fewer work challenges. They complete simpler tasks, like listening to voicemail rather than digging into deep project work. They also produce fewer creative solutions. They slack off. All this stuff is completely against what we're trying to do, reading this book and all. It's the opposite of productive, and this is what happens when we don't get adequate sleep.

All the signals of a lack of sleep in the workplace should be blowing up red signs, showing a lack of Ne going on. No deep work, no new ideas, nothing complicated, slacking off. It's the complete opposite of what we're trying to do here. Matthew Walker's conclusion was that less sleep doesn't equal productivity. In fact, he describes less sleep in the workplace as like being on a stationary bike. There might be movement, an image of looking busy, but the scene never changes. No one is making forward progress.

The consequences of sleep deprivation—which, again, he defines as less than eight hours—don't stop there. A lack of sleep causes a person to eat more, or at least to have the desire to eat more. When given the choice to eat anything they wanted from a premade buffet, the subjects who were more sleep-deprived, by and large, ate 200 more calories and made worse food choices, like sugary food and simple carbohydrates, than those who weren't sleep-deprived.

This conclusion that Dr. Walker drew is a little scary, and it's a theme you'll start to see popping up when you look deeper into the energy matrix. This is another reason why the energy matrix is a better metaphor than formula. In the matrix, the variables don't just sit on their own isolated plateaus but are intertwined, connected. In this instance, getting better sleep means you'll naturally make better food choices. The opposite is also true. Getting less-than-optimal sleep, you will be naturally inclined to make less-than-optimal food choices.

Food choices also affect sleep. Eating sugar is known to keep you up later at night and causes worse sleep. The energy matrix scares me because it's not very forgiving. If you mess up in one area, you seem to pay for it in another. However, stated more positively, if you do well in one area, you will see boosts in other areas of the matrix.

Ultimately, Dr. Walker's big conclusion about the importance of sleep is: The shorter your sleep, the shorter your life. This whole discipline and freedom thing just doesn't seem to go away, no matter where we look.

Strategies for Sleep

Okay, so you're convinced you need better sleep. How? The first and greatest thing you can do for yourself is achieve regularity. Fix your wake times. I don't go to sleep at the same time every day, but I do have an alarm that wakes me up at the same time. Regularity is the biggest thing you can do right from the start.

The next thing is lighting—not just the screen we stare at constantly throughout the day, but lighting everywhere. Having light after the sun goes down is unnatural. I know we're in the modern area and that's basically impossible. I was also a night auditor at a hotel for a year and a half when I was in school, so I used to go to sleep not long after 9 am. However, turning off the light is the next thing on the priority list of things to help you get

On Energy Management, Part 1

to sleep. The more lights you have on, the more you prevent the production of melatonin, the sleeping neurotransmitter. It's a simple one, and one you've probably heard of before if you've ever Googled "sleep habits" or "how to get better sleep," but too much light still stands high on the list of helpful habits for getting more sleep and, therefore, more energy.

Next is to keep it cool. The brain needs to be about two degrees Fahrenheit colder to initiate sleep. It's easier for people to fall asleep in a room that's too cold than in a room that's too hot. Sleeping semi-naked will do the trick, and hopefully you have control of the thermostat in your house. Thankfully, my wife and I both like a cool house, but in college, I had a difficult time when I roomed with a guy from Ethiopia. He was six-foot-one and weighed nighty pounds, and that's not an over-exaggeration—or under-exaggeration? And we fought constantly over the thermostat. Anyway, keep it cool.

There is something else to mention about the coolness of the body. Apparently, it helps if you keep your hands and feet warm, but the rest of your body cold. This coaxes the heat away from your core temperature. You want the surface of your body—and not your core temperature—to be warm. Another way to make this happen is through a warm bath. You may have heard some people say that taking a hot shower, or a warm bath, helps them go to sleep because their body is nice and warm, but the exact opposite is true. When you take a hot shower, your core temperature drops. When you get out, your core temperature is cool and the conditions are better for falling asleep.

The last thing is to listen to the Joe Rogan podcast during which he talks with Dr. Matthew Walker. It will seriously change your life and how you think about sleep. Or, better yet, go buy the bloke's book—*Why We Sleep: Unlocking the Power of Sleep and Dreams*.

CHAPTER 5:
ON ENERGY MANAGEMENT, PART 2

When I discussed the importance of sleep, I mainly used Dr. Matthew Walker's work and some the concepts from his book, *Why We Sleep: Unlocking the Power of Sleep and Dreams*. Now I'm going to talk about the exercise section of the matrix and its importance. Also, I'm going to use mainly one book that has had a profound effect on me in terms of my approach to exercise. It's a book by Dr. John J. Ratey called *Spark: The Revolutionary New Science of Exercise and the Brain*. If you want to learn more about exercise and the brain, I can't recommend a book more highly. I'm mostly going to summarize the book, focusing on the parts that surround the idea of energy.

Exercise

The book starts with a case study examining the effects of Naperville Central High School's Zero Hour program. The kids started the program at 7:10 am and exercised for thirty minutes before starting school. The kids either ran sprints, jumped rope, played tag, or played sports that involved cardiovascular activity. They wore heart rate monitors around their chests so the PE coach could record the level of activity for each student. Academically, the program's effects on the students were dramatic.

At the end of the semester, the kids who participated in the Zero Hour program showed an increase in reading comprehension of 17% compared to students of the high school who decided to take standard physical education and who increased their reading comprehension by only 10.7%. However, the increase in reading comprehension wasn't the thing that got Naperville High School national attention. It was when the school took the TIMSS, an international test that compares the science and math abilities of students around the world. TIMSS stands for "Trends in International Mathematics and Science Study." Naperville High School ended up ranking first in science. That's first in the world. In math, it ranked sixth, behind Singapore, Korea, Taiwan, Hong Kong, and Japan.

This was an incredible improvement over past international science and mathematics tests. Dr. Ratey explains that Naperville has the advantage of being an affluent suburb of Chicago. Generally, the high school did well in standardized tests compared to the rest of the country. However, when it ranked internationally on the TIMSS, it took its academic advantages to a whole new level.

On Energy Management, Part 2

I know this hasn't gotten to the science of exercise but it indicates that if you exercise, you will do better mathematically, scientifically, and ... readingly? The point is, you will learn better if you have an exercise routine.

In chapter 2, Dr. Ratey goes into the actual science of why this works. To summarize, he explains all the big parts of the brain that help it work, such as neurons, neurotransmitters, the cerebellum, the frontal cortex, the hippocampus, and all the different chemicals that circulate through the brain's circuitry. Basically, when you exercise, your entire body just works more efficiently, and that includes the brain. Your respiratory system brings oxygen to the brain more efficiently, and your circulatory system carries blood through the body, including the brain, more efficiently. Cells grow increasingly and effectively within the brain, and the different hormones and chemicals that allow you to learn new concepts are elevated. In particular, Dr. Ratey attributes cardiovascular exercise to brain health.

All this exercise, increased brain activity, and cell growth does more than simply help you learn more effectively. It helps with mood health as well. A study (known as the SMILE study) by James Blumenthal, and performed at Duke University, compared subjects who suffered from depression. One group used antidepressants and another group went through a controlled exercise routine. After the study, Dr. Blumenthal concluded that exercise had the same effect on mood as medication did. In the next chapter (chapter 6), he deals with the phenomenon of ADHD and makes a similar conclusion regarding Ritalin. The ADHD drug has the same effects as exercise.

I first read the book a few years ago, and ever since then, I haven't looked at exercise—and a way to get in shape—the same way. I consider it my medication. Like I said before, I've never been diagnosed with ADHD. My mother, with her natural way of curing everything, never would've allowed me to take drugs for a condition. Oh, pity me. I have, however, taken Adderall, though I'll talk about nootropics later in the chapter. I have been exercising for three to four times a week. Ever since I read this wonderful book, I have seen my exercise as fighting my depression and attention issues. I pop Ritalin and Prozac with cardio.

Besides all the mood health, exercise—specifically, any kind of movement—helps pump the lymphatic system. For a long time, we didn't know what pumped our lymph nodes. Blood is pumped through the heart, and oxygen to the lungs, but until recently we didn't know what pumped our bodies' waste. The lymphatic system rids our bodies of dead cells, bad bacteria, cancer cells, and toxins. Breathing and movement aren't the only ways to pump the lymphatic system but they're the best-known ways. And this happens through exercise. The benefits of exercise are so profound that in Canada, they are starting to use exercise as prescriptions for the elderly who profess depression-like symptoms.

Okay, so you're convinced. You need to start exercising. How do you go about doing that? Dr. Ratey's principal for brain-focus exercise follows a basic formula. Everything revolves around the heart rate. Figure out your maximum heart rate, then exercise somewhere between 50 to 85% of that zone. Your maximum heart rate is the number 220 minus your age. So, if you're 20 years old, your maximum heart rate is 200. If you're 20, your

On Energy Management, Part 2

maximum heart rate is 190. If you're 221 years old, your maximum heart rate is -1. You get the point.

Find any activity you want that keeps your heart rate at 50 to 85% of your maximum heart rate. Some examples are running, jogging, jumping rope, stair climbing, cycling, swimming, or Tony Robbins' trampoline thing. Just try anything that keeps your heart rate at an aerobic level. That's it. That's your Ritalin and Zoloft for the day.

Most of the scientific studies about exercise and the brain revolve around cardiovascular exercise. There isn't much said about body lifting—at least not a lot that I can find. But the heart rate principle still stands for bodybuilders. You may be a bodybuilder, but I'm going to go ahead and guess that you're not. Bodybuilding just doesn't seem like an INTP thing to do. If you are, great! I'd like to know your opinion about bodybuilding and brain function.

However, running seems to be a very "INTP" pastime. There are many different types of runners. Some people take it very competitively, but I think most INTPs are what is called a "Zen Runner." It's someone who gets out there and just lets his or her mind wander. I love to pop in some earphones and run while listening to just about anything: podcasts, audiobooks, music. Sometimes I just listen to whatever's running around in my head.

Anyway, if you like bodybuilding, I don't know much about it or the scientific literature on it. Most of everything that I've found and read comes from that *Spark* book and it focuses mostly on the heart principle.

That was only a slight dip into the exercise section of the matrix. Of course, you can get way deeper into the concept of exercise if you'd like, but I just want you to start doing something to improve your mental energy. Your Ne will thank you later for exercising, so get out there and do something.

On Meditation

Referring to the pretentious Plato quote at the beginning of the chapter, we already looked at how to achieve perfection through physical activity. Now it's time to venture into—and perfect—the mind.

Meditation is a difficult subject to talk about because of all the religious baggage that comes with it. There's a feeling of weirdness when someone says they meditate. It's like: "Ew. You're not one of the hippie, peace-on-earth, save-the-trees-type people, are you?" It's difficult to passively promote meditation because I'm instantly lumped in with all the weirdos trying to understand the "true self" and make intimate connections with the universe. Through meditation, I become one with everything. What? No. That's not what I'm trying to do at all. It's hard to get away from this strange stigma mainly because of the history of meditation.

A Brief History

No one really knows when the practice of meditation started. We find the earliest recordings about 3500 years ago, early in the Hindu religion, the oldest religion in the world. It seems that the concept of meditation has been around alongside religion. So, it should be no wonder that religion and meditation seem to go hand in hand. The practice has stuck around for a very long time, moving into other eastern religions such as Buddhism, Shinto, and many others.

It seems that prayer and contemplation—rather than clearing the mind—stuck around as the idea of meditation in the Abrahamic religions. I think this goes back to the deeper concepts of the eastern religions. Hinduism, a pantheistic religion, believes that everyone and everything is the God of the universe. Through meditation, you achieve this concept of escaping the wheel of life, Moksha in Hindu, Nirvana in Buddhism. It's like you connect yourself to the universe around you. You become one with it all, so to speak.

In a world religions course that I took in college, my teacher talked about Jain priests fasting and meditating until they withered away into nothingness. In my head, I was thinking, 'Yeah. Okay. They basically sat around meditating and then died of starvation. They didn't achieve enlightenment.' Maybe I was being judgmental. But this, I believe, was the basis for meditation in the beginning. Later, during the twentieth century, the practice made its way into the western world and we examined the phenomenon with our western eyes.

Jung studied the eastern religions during the 1920s and started a practice in his Bollingen Tower, his home, by setting up rooms dedicated solely to the practice of meditation. The Beatles and other pop stars popularized the practice in the 1960s, and from then on, universities started to study the practice, to see if there was anything to it. Dr. Herbert Benson is known as the pioneer in establishing the benefits of meditation. He researched the practice at Harvard University in the early 1970s and published numerous articles in scientific journals. Later, he published a book based on his studies, called *The Relaxation Response*, which is still in print today.

Benefits

Okay, so what are the benefits? There are a lot. It's hard to summarize all the benefits of meditation because some of them seem to come out of nowhere. However, we'll start things off with an excerpt from Dr. Jonathan's Haidt's book, *The Happiness Hypothesis*:

"Suppose you read about a pill that you could take once a day to reduce anxiety and increase your contentment. Would you take it? Suppose further that the pill has a great variety of side effects, all of them good: increased self-esteem, empathy, and trust; it even improves memory. Suppose, finally, that the pill is all natural and costs nothing. Now would you take it?

The pill exists. It's called meditation."

These aren't all the benefits of the meditation pill, but they're some of them. He lists: 1) self-esteem, 2) lower anxiety, 3) increased contentment, 4) empathy, 5) trust (kind of a weird benefit), and 6) memory.

I'll start to add more to this list. Another benefit is an improved immune system. Harvard Medical School discovered this one. They found that practitioners of meditation have higher mitochondrial energy production, meaning the body's cellular ecosystem is much healthier.

The University of Kentucky came up with a study that showed that meditators, even beginners, needed less sleep than those who had no meditation practice.
https://www.ncbi.nlm.nih.gov/pmc/articles/PMC2919439/

This isn't to say that meditation will replace your sleep; rather, you will simply require less if you make a practice of settling into a meditative state sometime during the day.

Another weird benefit is an improved sense of touch. Researchers at the Ruhr-University Bochum and the Ludwig-Maximilians-University München proved this one. Meditation improved the subject's sense of touch by 17%! Wow! You have to be convinced now! A better sense of TOUCH! Think about all the things you could touch better through the practice of meditation! You could touch more carpets, tables, cats, or homeless people! You see, meditation opens up entirely new worlds!

The University of Rome did some studies on meditation and creativity. And, yes, it also boosts creativity.

https://www.ncbi.nlm.nih.gov/pmc/articles/PMC3887545/

Your brain, during meditation, lowers its activity to alpha and theta waves. For some reason, the muse's voice is louder and clearer when the mind is calm. Things just come to us when our minds are farthest away from the fight-or-flight stimulation of the brain and body. Look at the Buddha, for example. If you don't know the story, the Buddha was deep in the woods for forty days when the idea of enlightenment hit him. He got this "eureka" moment after settling his mind into the deep theta waves of the brain—the same waves our brains produce when we are in the dreaming stage of sleep. Meditation helps us stay in the calm state, which allows us to produce more interesting ideas.

Last but certainly not least, meditation improves attention. More specifically, it helps one bring his or her attention back to a task. It was the University of Minnesota that established this one.

https://journals.plos.org/plosone/article?id=10.1371/journal.pone.0003083

The researchers discovered that practitioners of meditation were better able to drop extraneous thoughts and return to the subject at hand, be it breathing, reading, writing, or dancing naked in the snow. Meditation helps one increase the ability to control his or her focus. It helps one return his or her mind to the task at hand. Basically, it increases one's attention.

Meditation was also shown to increase grey matter in the brain, in areas associated with learning, memory, and emotion. https://www.ncbi.nlm.nih.gov/pmc/articles/PMC3004979/

So, meditation actually grows the brain. Your brain gets bigger with meditation, which makes for a great argument that meditation is exercise for the brain. With meditation, for every function that the brain performs, everything simply gets better.

Why Does It Work?

On Energy Management, Part 2

This is a difficult question to ask because meditation is centered around the brain, and the brain is the body's most mysterious organ. We know less about it than about any other organ in the body. I was listening to a neurologist on the radio talk about how little we know about the brain. He used an outer space metaphor to explain our knowledge of this three-pound organ. He said that it's like we're looking at the earth from a satellite, but we really have no idea what's underneath the surface. The brain oversees every single function of the body. Answer me this: What does the body do that the brain is somehow not in charge of? It does everything.

Once I woke up from a dream during the night. In the dream, a candle was burning my arm and it really hurt. It really, really hurt, and I mean, it physically hurt. I woke up and my arm was still burning, still physically hurting like it had during the dream, and I could find no physical explanation for this. I wasn't lying on it or doing anything that would cause this painful, burning sensation on the surface of my skin. Now, what was causing my arm to burn? I've heard many other stories like this, about the things the brain can do, which seems to completely defy the logic of the material world. Placebo effects are a real thing. It's a crazy phenomenon if you sit back and think about it.

In college, there was a kid to whom some friends of mine gave fake beer. He drank several cans of the fake beer. I can't remember quite how much but he ended up sloppy drunk in about an hour. He was slurring his words and stumbling over himself. Then he was told that the beer was fake. He didn't believe it and still had this sunken, dead look in his eyes, like he wasn't all there, like the way drunk people normally look.

I'm just saying that we have no idea how the brain works, though meditation seems to help it in only positive ways. Every function that it performs seems to increase and improve with meditation. It's really difficult to sit here and tell you everything that meditation helps with in the brain, because there's so much about the brain—and, therefore, meditation—we don't know.

The Exercise

So, you're convinced you need to start a meditation practice. Good. Maybe you already have a meditation practice and want to simply review the benefits and the process of meditation. Also good. Or maybe you're just interested in the process and are flirting with the idea, which I would consider also good. You're pursuing things that interest you.

Okay, so how do you meditate? There are thousands of ways. There are so many different types of meditation: mindfulness, transcendental, compassion, mantra, yoga, "I am," Daoist, and all the different guided meditations sprinkled throughout the pages of the internet. You can do your own research on meditation but I want to boil down the important parts of the practice.

The first principle, I would say, is movement. You have to find a spot and not move—like, literally not move for as long as the session takes. Your brain normally follows the body, so to get into a deep, calm, meditative state, the body can't move, or the brain has to use its energy for every single movement. Any type of movement prevents the brain from getting into those deep levels of consciousness. So, find a position to sit in where you won't

On Energy Management, Part 2

have to move for a long period of time, or however long you wish to meditate. This is easier said than done.

I meditate in my car all the time and I find my legs falling asleep if they're set in just the slightest awkward position. I'll sit down and think, 'Oh, that seems good,' and then five minutes into the session, my leg falls asleep. So, find a position in which you will not have to move for the meditation session.

Next is posture. One piece of good advice that I heard online—I can't remember where—was to sit with dignity. When sitting, or if you have one of those cool yoga positions down, sit with your back straight and as if you were being super formal at a banquet or something. I normally have my head against a wall or against a high-backed chair, because my head will wobble forward and backward, which is movement, which isn't good.

Next is anchoring. This is what all meditation techniques have in common. The anchors are always the weird, mystical thing that creeps people out, and I can understand why. In the Shinto religion, one has to meditate over the names of the evil spirits so they'll move away from that person's house. Otherwise, the evil spirits will take over, and bad things will start to happen. Transcendental Meditation makes all its money from the mantra. It says that everyone must be given their own mantra, made specifically for them. The person must not tell anyone what the mantra because then it will lose its power.

Science hasn't been able to understand all the stuff except in the context of fraud. Honestly, I think the TM community would lose all its business if it didn't take the anchor so seriously. People pay thousands of dollars for the mantra. However, the studies reveal that the anchors aren't important. It's only important that you have an anchor.

An anchor is basically something you keep returning to when your mind wanders. It can be either your breath, a mantra, or someone's voice guiding you through a meditation session. The true exercise of any meditation session is to bring your focus back to the anchor.

It'll go something like this. Say your anchor is your breath. You're focusing on it. You can feel your stomach push out as you inhale, and then shrink as you let the air out of your lungs. You pay attention to this cycle of inhaling and exhaling for maybe thirty seconds, and you think, 'Hmm. I need to go to the store. I forgot to buy...' And you lost your focus on your breath. Hey! Great job! You noticed that your mind wandered. Now it's time to get in another rep and bring the focus back to the anchor. You bring it back to the anchor and you lose focus again. This happens throughout the entire process.

A word on frustration: Don't. Okay, that was my word on frustration. Don't. Seriously, don't get frustrated that you keep wandering. You shouldn't expect to focus on the anchor for 50% of the session. If you focus on your anchor for 15%, that's a good session. They say to not judge a meditation session and I agree. Try your best to not judge it, and if you do really bad, take it as a sign that you need to meditate more and to not give it up because your mind is all over the place. Some great advice that I learned from the good people of the internet is to think of it like a brushing-of-the-teeth session. Do you ever get done brushing your teeth and think, 'Wow. What a horrible job I did. Man, that

On Energy Management, Part 2

sucked. I'm going to quit brushing my teeth because I'm not getting the results I wanted.' No one ever thinks like that—at least no one I know.

To summarize the practice: 1) Have a good, dignified posture. 2) Don't move. 3) Find an anchor and stick with it. 4) Judge not like ye not judge brushing teeth.

Other Options in the Matrix

I talked with one of my friends about the idea of the energy matrix, and he really liked it, except for the meditation part. He felt it was a little arbitrary and that if meditation was on there, affirmations and the like should be on there as well. I did, and still do, agree with him at some level. However, affirmations don't seem to have the same scientific backing as meditation does. And I can't find the benefits of affirmation to be as all-encompassing as those of meditation. Therefore, I decided to leave that off along with many other habits that seem to help other very successful people.

I encourage you, if you have other things you'd like to place on the matrix, go for it. Put your goal for affirmations on there and measure it, but I wouldn't take off any of the four I have there. You'd be missing out on the huge energy-related benefits that each of the four variables provides. However, here are some other options to help you increase the energy tank.

The Wim Hof Method

You may have heard about this guy. If you haven't, the words "Wim Hof" should be the next things you put into the Google search engine. The guy currently, as of 2019, holds twenty-six world records that range from taking the longest ice bath to climbing to the highest altitude on Mount Everest wearing nothing but shorts and shoes to swimming the longest distance under iced-over water—57.5 m. (188 ft 6in).

His method is basically controlled hyperventilation. You flood your body with oxygen, giving the body several side effects. One, the alkalinity levels of the body increase. I can really tell a difference when I drink too much coffee. I normally drink mine black, with no cream or milk or anything. Black coffee is very acidic, and when I follow his method I can feel the inflammation in my shoulder decrease. I have some nerve damage from the military. Often, I follow his method simply because it helps my shoulder, not for the energy.

It may be better if you watched a YouTube video of someone doing the technique, but I'll do my best to explain the process. Before I explain it, don't do this in water or while standing up. Some people have passed out while doing this technique. One guy was doing the method in a body of water, passed out, and drowned. So, find a safe place before you begin, in case you pass out.

It goes something like this:

1. Find someplace safe to sit or lie down.

2. Breathe in, expanding the stomach until you feel tension in your solar plexus. It's an area at the upper end of the stomach.
3. Don't push the air out; just let it fall out on its own.
4. Breathe in the same way. You should start to feel a little stressed and lightheaded. Your body should be telling you, "Hey, stop! That's way too much oxygen! You don't need all of this!" Force your breath anyway.
5. Go through the cycle of breathing in and letting the air out twenty to twenty-five times.

This is the fun part. All the earlier stuff stresses me out.

6. Push every bit of oxygen out of your body, and then hold your breath for as long as possible.
7. When you start to panic or you just can't hold your breath any longer, breathe in as much oxygen as you can and hold it for twenty seconds. You should start to feel a tingling sensation in your body.

And that's it. Once you're done, you should feel lightheaded. Wim Hof suggests doing the method three or four times. However, you can look up the rest of his stuff on your own if you're interested. I like to do exercises during the no-oxygen phase. Some people do pushups, but I'm worried I'll fall on my face and break my nose if I pass out. I do squats or lunges instead.

Strategies for Naps

Another technique for energy is napping. The workplace is starting to understand the power of naps. In Tokyo, there are little napping shops, called napping salons or napping capsules.

The basic rule for napping is 20 minutes—60 minutes —90 minutes. You can take a nap for that amount of time but anything past those sweet spots and you'll fall into a phase of sleep called sleep inertia, where it becomes very difficult to rouse yourself after the nap. You'll carry around grogginess that will be difficult to shake. For the twenty-minute rule, you can get up before then. Somewhere between ten minutes and twenty minutes is good. You probably won't fall asleep, but sleep isn't the point. It's a time to let your mind take a break and wander. It's not meditation because meditation is an exercise, while napping is rest.

Another really fun technique is the coffee nap. If you've never tried coffee napping, I highly recommend it. It takes caffeine ten to twenty minutes to start doing its magic. So, the logic goes, take a shot of caffeine and then close your eyes for between ten and twenty minutes. When you get up, you'll be in a state of calm alertness that everyone is trying to get into. You see, we don't want to be super calm to the point that we're tired, and we don't want to be super vigilant so that we can't control ourselves. Instead, we want to be somewhere between those two states. And a coffee nap is one answer. I highly, highly recommend it.

Another energy technique is a little controversial, especially if my wife is in the conversation. She hates that I do this. I don't smoke. I never have, but I do chew Nicorette gum whenever I want a dopamine hit. In fact, as I'm writing this, I have some Nicorette gum tucked into the side of my jaw. It's controversial. From the studies I've glanced over, the big worry about nicotine is about when someone decides to switch to cigarettes or if the person using nicotine products is underage. It does cause prefrontal cortex impairment.

But … but … but … there are also studies showing that nicotine can help protect the brain, warding off early signs of Alzheimer's and Parkinson's. So, if you're past the age of 18 and use too much caffeine, and if you don't already smoke or use nicotine, try using Nicorette. Before, I talked about how Ne is centered around dopamine. Well, one cheap way to get a quick hit of dopamine is through Nicorette gum. If you do smoke, I'm sure you know about all the health risks and that's your choice. As for Nicorette gum, it seems to be the equivalent of drinking coffee. It's just another way for me to get a bit of energy to make it through the day.

The Energy Matrix Revisited

That just about does it for me and this energy matrix idea. Set goals for yourself and learn these habits. Other types may tell you to be productive by keeping a daily schedule, and I don't want to knock the idea of a schedule. Sometimes I keep a schedule and other times I don't. In the next chapter, I will go over scheduling and also over the idea of why it's so difficult to schedule your day as an INTP. Coming up with a schedule isn't the difficult part; rather, it's the energy it takes to follow through. It will be much, much easier—like much, much easier—if you have established good habits to improve your energy. I can't stress how important it is for you to work on increasing your energy tank.

Other types may have more discipline than we do when it comes to scheduling their day and following through with that schedule, but that will be their discipline. They don't have the crazy Ne function that seeks to explore new ideas and interesting concepts. They aren't going to work as hard at understanding all the different concepts floating around in the realm of ideas. Understanding the stuff we want to get into requires loads of energy. And having loads of energy requires discipline on our part. So, learn to break your bad habits and learn the habits of creating energy. Your Ne will thank you for it.

As the underlying principle goes, the more energy you have, the more the world of possibilities will be opened to you. As discussed earlier, the opposite also holds true. The more bad habits that creep into your life, the more those possibilities start to disappear. Through discipline comes that precious thing all we INTP would die for and kill ourselves if we didn't have: freedom. Now it's time to enter the energy matrix.

CHAPTER 6:
ON TIME MANAGEMENT

Now, because you've mastered the energy matrix AND discovered interests that are calling your name, you need some strategies to help plan your day. You've probably listened to advice from others and planned your day vigorously, tacking in every minute of the day, or at least every hour. Maybe it worked out great for the first day.

When I was in college, a podcast dedicated to people with ADHD gave me the advice to schedule every single hour of my day, and so I tried it. The night before, I had everything on a sheet of paper, from when I woke up until about 3 pm. I started the day and I utterly destroyed everything, getting through all my school projects way faster than I expected. I was like, "Whoa ... This really works." I felt as if I was on pace to conquering the world in the next three to four years.

The next day, I followed the schedule again. I planned my entire day and I did okay. I got some of the tasks done, but it felt like I was killing my soul. Something inside me was pulling me away from my college reading or writing papers I had due in the coming weeks. I'm not sure what it was. Everything was so predictable and set in stone, and my being was like, "Are you going to do this for the rest of your life? Trap yourself inside a schedule like this?" I might as well have been an android moving from one task to another. It was as if I'd given up my right to be a human being. I couldn't handle it anymore. Just like the night before, I made a schedule for myself for the next day ... and I avoided it all day and did absolutely nothing.

One day, I was on pace to conquering the world in the next three to four years and the next I was on pace to failing college, quitting my job, and being homeless for the rest of my life. I asked myself, "Who am I?" Seriously, I didn't know. One day I felt like Genghis Khan and the next day I felt like the bum on the corner, urinating in his pants. How was I supposed to look at myself? Was I the super-productive world beater on pace to world domination? Or was I the person with no future, set to live in the slums with all my homeless friends? I was on either one side or the other. I couldn't find the predictable world in between.

Then I thought: Did I really want to be in that zone of predictable, consistent productivity? No, I really didn't. I didn't, and still don't, want to know what I can get done in a day. At the time, I didn't really have the language to express what I was going through. Later in life, the world of MBTI gave me a lens and a language for understanding why I had trouble sticking with a schedule consistently.

The Problem with Scheduling

You, as an INTP, have probably followed the advice of others and created a daily schedule of your own. What's interesting is that you've probably always liked the idea of a schedule but at the

On Time Management

same time, when the schedule for your day was sitting in front of you, you hated it. In college and throughout life, I have bounced all over the place, trying to figure out the daily schedule. I admire the people who do keep schedules for themselves but my hatred for schedules grows as the ever-increasing to-do list extends with each task.

The problem can be explained using the Si and Ne functions. They are at war within you. One function would really like the structure of a task, Si, and wants you to follow through with it. Si isn't a creative function. It relies on Ne to give it new information. It's very underdeveloped, so it doesn't have quite as much say when it comes to sticking to a task. However, you can hear her scream when you set a flame under the paper describing the things you need to do. You don't want to do it anymore. She takes all the information of the day and holds you to it.

The problem is Ne and Si. Ne is the exact opposite function and wants to try new ideas. It's the function that carried you through the first couple of days on your schedule. The problem on day three or four was that Ne felt as if he'd already figured out the daily schedule, so he didn't care for it. He wanted to try something new. He was bored. Unfortunately, Ne is the function that pulls an INTP forward. You must have something interesting pulling you in the outside, or inside, world.

As I explained, Ne and Si are the exact opposite functions, just like Ti and Fe are the exact opposite. One function is intuition, the other is sensing. One function is introverted, the other is extroverted. They put their energy in opposite directions, so it's very difficult to get them on board with something.

A very accurate way of looking at them is like the yin and yang symbol, but with absolutely no dots of the opposite color inside either of the shades. One side is completely black and the other is completely white.

So, what do you do? Somehow, they must work together. That's what the rest of the chapter is about.

Si and Predictability

I've learned a lot about Si through my wife. She's an ISFJ and leads with the function. She's constantly in Si, needing to have everything in its place at all times. She has a difficult time handling anomalies. She'll admit this. If something isn't in its place, she freaks out.

My parents are coming to town sometime in June but due to circumstances, we don't know when they'll be here exactly. My wife is freaking out a little bit because she wants to know, in her head, exactly when and how everything will be. When will they get here? When will they leave? What room are they going to stay in? How are we going to do this with only one bathroom? Si is crying out for structure and predictability because she leads with the function; her Si is super, super developed. It really baffles me how developed her Si is. I watch her plan her day, which I will get to later, and she actually does it, and does it consistently.

My wife will tell me that she likes to think ahead. Though I think this is partly true, I also think a large part of her is trying to prevent the unexpected from happening. Planning ahead and thinking of everything that might go wrong helps her push away all chances of unwanted surprises.

Personally, I have both disdain and admiration for the function Si. I work with an ISTJ, my mother's an ISFJ, and I have an ESTJ brother. Any SJ type will have Si somewhere in the primary or secondary spot. I do like knowing what's going on around me and keeping a database of information I have gathered from the Ne function.

But Ne is a big problem. Like Ti suppresses Fe, Ne suppresses Si. The Ne function wants this predictability to go away. So, how are you to hold yourself to a perfectly predictable day when you have this stronger disdain for it? The more you plan your day, the more the possibilities of it disappear. What's the fun in that?

Ne and Possibilities

I recently read a biography of Walt Disney. Throughout the book, I kept analyzing his personality type. Most people online agree that he was an ENFP and I highly agree after reading *Walt Disney: The Triumph of the American Imagination*. The guy's Ne was off the charts. When making the film *Snow White and the Seven Dwarfs*, he never conclusively made a decision. Everything he said was open for change, and it drove the animators and storytellers insane. He was constantly thinking about the directions in which the movie could go, or what the characters would look like. He was always thinking, 'It could be this … or no. It could be like this!' Thinking of possibilities was the theme of Walt Disney's entire life, with all the good and the bad that Ne brings.

However, always being in a world of possibilities is a problem for Ne. The function never really wants to make a conclusive statement about anything. Once you fully decide on an idea (or, in this case, a daily schedule), there's nothing for the Ne to do. It's done. It moves on. Or, worse, it wishes to destroy what's been set in stone, to see if he can break it.

Philip K. Dick, in the essay I quoted from earlier, "How to Build a Universe That Doesn't Fall Apart Two Days Later," says, "However, I will reveal a secret to you: I like to build universes which do fall apart. I like to see them come unglued, and I like to see how the characters in the novels cope with this problem. I have a secret love of chaos. There should be more of it." Underneath the calm façade of every INTP, I believe there is a secret love for chaos, a desire for things to not go the way they're supposed to go.

When I was young, I told my mother that I liked it whenever the power went out. She thought I was crazy, and she still does. The power going out is like a break from the machine of life. Everything is going as it's supposed to go, the power plants are churning out electricity, my computer is working, and people are going about their day as if things will continue to work and always work. But then something happens that gets in the way—an anomaly that says underneath all the seemingly solidified structure is a vulnerability about which very few people think. The vulnerability is exposed. A squirrel chews on a power line and electricity, the very thing upon which modern societies are built, goes away and society stops. The universe falls apart —but only for a moment.

On Time Management

This is a reason why it's very difficult to make a schedule. Before we desire everything to be set in place and predictable, there is a desire for everything to fall apart. The question is, is it possible to make a daily schedule with this desire for chaos, this desire for things to not go the way they're supposed to go? I believe so. I believe there's a way to get both Ne and Si working together.

Chaos and Order

The answer to this question, I believe, lies within the yin and yang symbol. I stated that Ne and Si are exact opposites, and that a great way to think about them is with the image of the yin and yang symbol. One represents chaos and the other order. Jordan Peterson, in his book, *12 Rules for Life*, has a chapter explaining the rule: "Pursue What Is Meaningful and Not What Is Expedient." In it, he states that the place of meaning is standing with one foot in chaos and one foot in order, one opposite dot in each color. Si and Ne must have the seeds of each other inside them. Si can't be fully order, while Ne can't be fully chaos.

Yeah, cool, that's an interesting theory and all, but how would that work? In practice, you're going to have to find a balance for yourself. You must find how much structure you can handle. That's really the key to having a schedule.

I've discovered the answers for myself, and I've developed strategies from the idea, but this is the underlying principle that holds my scheduling system together. When I start to feel as though my days have solidified, I basically throw away my schedule and make a new one.

It's not the most efficient way of pursuing my day, and I accept that because I have such a difficult time knowing exactly what I'm going to do every single day. I see how much order I can impose on my Ne and I back off when I feel as if I'm losing my soul. Yes, I base a lot of my scheduling on feeling. When I start to feel trapped, when my soul starts to dissipate into nonexistence, I back off and make a completely new schedule. Let's get into how this is done.

Start with a Vision

You have to remember that creating a schedule is a skill and it won't come easily at first. It still doesn't come easily to me. However, before you begin making a schedule, you need some kind of vision. You have to ask yourself, "What kind of day do I want?" What do you want to get done? What do you want to do? Sometimes I complete this process by writing it down freely on a piece of paper. Having a vision starts with Ne, which you'll eventually give to your Si to schedule and to hold you to it. This process may take some time.

One of the things I worry about when developing a vision for my day is whether I will have enough energy to complete what I want to complete. You'll never know how much energy you'll have until you're inside the day's forest, making your way through the trees, making your own paths.

Right now, as you develop a vision, you are looking at the entire day from a 10,000-foot view. It's the big picture. Your Ne is coming up with all sorts of ideas and possibilities and "What if?" questions. What could I do? What could I get done? You'll never

On Time Management

fully know the answer to that, which is what makes each day interesting.

You'll never know how much you can get done. Sometimes it's less than expected and sometimes it's more. But without having a vision for the day, without using your imagination, you'll have no idea where you're going. The next day, you'll be in the forest, meandering around, not sure where you're going, and you'll find your place in the same area at the end of the day.

Ne and Si Together

Next, when you have an idea of what you'd like to get done, write it down. And write it down by hand. You can put it on your computer, or in an app on your phone, but I highly discourage this. I seriously doubt that you'll check your phone as much as you'd check a piece of paper sitting in front of you, with the day's tasks staring at you, constantly unchecked.

If you notice how SJs plan their day, you'll see that they generally don't plan in a sequence of time, like Ni users do. I highly suggest writing only a to-do list. Si doesn't keep track of time, what has and has not been completed. Si is a database, not a time schedule. Most SJs, at least those whom I know, simply make a to-do list to structure their day. This is what I need to get done for the day. So, make a to-do list for your Si, and not a time schedule. This is the fun part of the to-do list: You can complete any task you want. You look over your to-do list and think, 'What's the next thing I'd like to work on?' Asking this question engages your Ne. What could I do next? You ask the question, you get an answer, and then you do it. Remember, this is INTP advice. Most other types wouldn't tell you to structure your day like this because, well, this isn't very structured. And that's the point.

This will inevitably happen. It's not good when it does, but it'll happen a lot, especially in the beginning, if you haven't mastered the skill of the to-do list. You'll go down rabbit holes, on YouTube, or Wikipedia, or Google, or whatever fits your fancy. You have completely lost your momentum, and yet this to-do list is sitting next to you, full of things that you no longer want to do. That's fine. You can start the process all over again. Make a vision, make a to-do list, and move through the tasks.

To prevent myself from getting overwhelmed, whenever I have to restart my day, I simply write down three things. Once I do them, the momentum is back and then I can write down more things.

The process must be fluid, malleable. You must give yourself the luxury of rewriting your vision throughout the day. Once you're in the day, in the forest, you start to see what you're really getting yourself into. At any moment throughout the day, you can stop and throw your to-do list into the trash, and then make a new one. This keeps you from feeling trapped as you move from one task to the next. You've given yourself the freedom to rewrite your to-do list whenever you want. It's not complete freedom, but it's enough.

And if I start to feel trapped, or if the to-do list isn't getting me where I want to go, or if I have a change of plans, I simply take the piece of paper, crumple it up, throw it away, and make a new one. Some days I'll go through this process three or four times, while other days I do exactly what I set out to do from the beginning.

On Time Management

Tiny Steps

It's very important to write down small tasks to complete. The smaller the task, the less anxiety you'll have about whatever it is you're trying to do.

You may have heard of the psychological therapy called Aversion Therapy. It's a therapy that helps people move toward things that scare them. One way to help prevent feelings of anxiety is to approach the source of that anxiety in small steps. As an English major, I had to write many papers in school. If I wrote, "Write twelve-page paper" on my to-do list, that would have completely overwhelmed me.

You want to think like an aversion therapist for yourself and come up with the next step you can take toward completing the twelve-page paper, or whatever project you're working on, or whatever thing you want to do. For the paper, maybe my next step would be "Look up twelve articles about the idea I want to write about." But maybe that's too much. Maybe I don't even know where to look up articles. That becomes the next thing on the to-do list. I write, "Find a database to look up articles." The next step would be, "Find one article about INTP personalities."

Often, I never return to the to-do list because simply writing it down helps clarify my vision of what I want to accomplish. However, the principle to remember here is: The smaller the step, the less anxiety you will feel. Break down the task and put it on a to-do list.

Where to Keep Your List

Hopefully, by now you're convinced to create a vision for your day and make a list of steps toward whatever it is you're trying to accomplish. You may have some ideas about where to keep your to-do list, but I highly suggest staying away from electronics. You can experiment with apps if you like, but the thing about electronics is that there is very little that triggers you to review the list. Maybe completing a task triggers you, but returning to the to-do list is actually very difficult. Therefore, you want to make it as easy as possible for you to look back at the list.

Basically, write it down on a piece of paper. I know, unfortunately, you aren't that aware of the world around you, so you aren't going to look at the list very often unless you've figured out something that I haven't. However, when you keep a list in the physical world, on a physical piece of paper, it will always sit there and stare at you and judge you for the tasks you haven't completed. If you keep your to-do list on your phone, the list disappears every time you turn off the phone. It goes away and you have no awareness of it. On the other hand, a list sitting on the desk, next to your computer, will remain there until you either throw it away or make and complete a new one.

I've written to-do lists for all sorts of things. I've written them on printing paper, napkins, sticky notes, and small notepads. You can write down what needs to be done on anything that has a flat surface and that can hold ink or pencil marks. I've developed a routine of using these little notepads I bought from Walmart. They're, like, two bucks for five of them and one pad lasts me for several months. If you make a to-do list, you have to ask yourself, "What's going to bring me back to the list?" You have to be honest with this question. I've tried maybe a hundred (honestly,

On Time Management

about a dozen) electronic to-do lists on the computer, or on my iPhone, or on Google Chrome, and none of them worked like a piece of paper sitting in my immediate work environment.

Throughout the day, I'll start to feel lost. I don't know where I am, and I don't know where to go. I had this huge vision for the day that I wanted to get done, but I can't remember any of it. So I simply look down and there's a list of things that need to be done, and I work on one.

Scheduling Summary

You've probably experimented with several different ways to schedule your day, but couldn't consistently stick with the habit because it was too stifling. You felt trapped. It took away too much freedom. Your Ne was no longer pulling you forward. Yet at the same time, you wished to find a scheduling process that would work. You wanted to find a strategy. This was your tiny Si voice speaking. You want freedom and you want to lock yourself into a set schedule. How is that even possible? How can someone have these opposing desires? All types have their paradoxes, and this is just one of the conflicting desires of the INTP.

Somehow you have to get your Si and Ne to work together. Start by developing a vision. Look at the forest of the day from a 10,000-foot view, and think, 'What do you want to get done? At the end of the day, what could I look back at and be proud of?' Then write it down on a physical piece of paper and make the steps small so that you aren't overwhelmed. If you are overwhelmed, you aren't thinking small enough. Tasks should be tiny enough for you to move forward.

Make a to-do list and not a time schedule. Work on any task that will move you toward the destination. If you feel trapped, then burn the list and develop another vision. Remember, you can burn the list whenever you want, but you must make a new one. If you go down a rabbit hole and can't find a moment to get yourself back on task, just make another vision for the day whenever you want. This keeps the day's schedule fluid, which helps engage both your desire to have a schedule, Si, and your desire to explore the unknown, Ne.

Now go and develop a vision for the rest of your day. Put the skill into practice.

Printed in Poland
by Amazon Fulfillment
Poland Sp. z o.o., Wrocław